PRAYER WORKS
BUT I NEED
A PRESCRIPTION

PRAYER WORKS BUT I NEED A PRESCRIPTION

A PERSONAL JOURNEY THROUGH DISCOVERY, AWARENESS, AND MANAGEMENT OF MENTAL HEALTH

RONSHANTA WASHINGTON

PRAYER WORKS BUT I NEED A PRESCRIPTION
*A personal journey through discovery, awareness,
and management of mental health*

The information in this book is based on the author's
knowledge, experience, and opinions. The ideas and methods
described in this book are not intended to be a definitive set of
instructions. You may discover other methods and materials to
accomplish the same end result. Your results may differ.

Paperback ISBN: 979-8-218-41421-4
First Paperback Edition: May 2024

Edited by: Khloe's Thoughts Editing
Cover by: Make Your Mark Publishing Solutions
Layout by: Make Your Mark Publishing Solutions

CONTENTS

ACKNOWLEDGEMENTS

First and foremost, I would like to give thanks to my Lord and Savior Jesus Christ. In my time of need and all that I have experienced mentally and emotionally, God has been my foundation and the only thing that has not wavered in my life.

With that being said, I thank my mother, Monica Faye Cox, and my father, Ronald Lewis, along with my grandmother, Dorothy Washington. They have played a crucial role in my belief and faith in God. They introduced me to God, prayer, and his word. When I told my father I was writing a book about how he and my mother messed me up (jokingly of course), he replied, "Well, you should have a New York Times Best seller!" I took it as encouragement and approval.

Thank you to my talented and extremely knowledgeable publishing coach, Monique Mensah, and amazing editor, Khloe Cain. Special thanks to my beautiful daughter Jaelyn, who encouraged me early on to continue writing. She knew friends who could benefit from my story. Finally, thank you to my husband, Tyrone Mitchell, who read the whole manuscript and looked at every book cover design several times and assured me it would bless many people.

DEDICATION

To both my parents, the woman I am today
is because of you two. Thank you!

And to anyone who has struggled with their mental health,
you can, you have, and you are surviving! Keep fighting!

INTRODUCTION

Life has a peculiar way of reminding you of lessons you haven't grasped yet, trauma you haven't confronted, and realities you refuse to accept. This is for the little girl within me that I struggle to heal a little every day. For every parent who has felt misunderstood and hurt by their child, forgive them. They are unaware of the deeply rooted pain that is embedded within the family unit like a 100-year-old tree with roots seven feet deep, underground, invisible to the eye. Most people see their parents in the form of a superhero who has it all together and can or should do no wrong. When in reality, they are human beings just like us, who were once children and experienced their own pain and struggles in life.

For every daughter and son who has felt mishandled by their mother or father, forgive them. It's not easy caring for a child while carrying the burden of your own unresolved trauma. Unresolved trauma does not just go away. It shows up in some shape, form, or fashion. For myself, I became highly anxious, followed by depression and several other physical symptoms such as tremors. I struggled to under-stand it. I tried to hide it. I refused to accept it. I tried to control it. I tried to suppress it. But it refused to leave. It was like it had become a part of me. Then one day, I finally decided to confront it!

This book tells the story of how I confronted my mental health, analyzed my childhood, accepted who I am, and began to heal and become the best version of myself.

"ANXIETY DOES NOT EMPTY TOMORROW OF ITS SORROWS, BUT ONLY EMPTIES TODAY OF ITS STRENGTH."

-CHARLES SPURGEON

SELF-AWARENESS

SO MUCH IN my life has changed yet so many things have stayed the same. I feel like a bigger complicated version of the child that I once was. I'm an adult woman, struggling with the emotional insecurities I felt as a child while attempting to mask my loud but silent tears. Every day seems like a struggle but also a learning experience as I continue to grow and discover myself. Some days I feel what society tells me is "normal" and other days I feel so out of place, that I can barely function. Yet, I still have to be a mother. I still have to work my stressful job and my newest role as a wife. Some days I'm able to ease through my day gracefully with my thoughts and movements under control and I encourage myself along the way and say, "hey you're doing good." Then that little annoying voice starts to whisper and a small part of me starts to panic inside. As self-doubt creeps in, I began to question myself and wonder, am I really doing good? What if something goes wrong? As my mind starts to fill in the blanks, I attempt positive self-talk reminding myself how strong and intelligent I am. Whatever I may be doing or wherever I'm at, I'm more than capable of handling what's in my path. There is no real threat present, and I reassure myself that this is my mind trying to play tricks on me. Some days I can redirect that little voice and tune it out. Other days it takes over me, consumes me, and I feel like I'm drowning, and no one even sees me.

I remember being a respiratory care student, attending hospital clinicals afraid and scared daily. I would usually arrive early enough to sit in my car and gather my nerves and pray before I walked into the hospital. I thought to myself how will I ever get through this being afraid the way I am? I wondered if people noticed my fear fighting for custody of my mind and my body. My first clinical site was at the Northwest Community Hospital in Arlington Heights, Illinois. My preceptor told myself and two other students, "You are allowed to make any and all mistakes as long as you don't kill anyone. Don't be afraid to ask questions, try everything, and take advantage of every opportunity in front of you. This is an environment to learn hands on you're not expected to know everything." One of my classmates did exactly that, he seemed so confident and eager. He was the first to volunteer to do everything! I was the total opposite. As for myself, I was still afraid and everything I did was done cautiously while moving in fear. It wasn't necessarily a bad thing because I was still trying. However, it was so much more I could've experienced and learned hands on had I just been able to get out of my own way! Even when being told I didn't have to be perfect and it was okay to make a mistake, I still hesitated and wanted to appear perfect, which meant play it safe. I didn't want to look incompetent.

As a student, I didn't have a state license to protect me yet. I wasn't expected to know everything. I was there to learn through observation, hands on, and ask questions like he told me. Once again, fear was my tour guide and dictated what areas I was allowed to partake in and when enough was enough. While everyone else was just going with the flow I was trying to control the flow, predict outcomes, calculate movements while treading lightly. I started slowly losing control during that whole experience. I now know it was and seems to always be the fear of failure and embarrassment exaggerated by my anxiety. Even when I'm doing well, that little voice whispers are you really doing well or okay? So, even when I knew I deserved to be there I questioned my capabilities.

Life is full of learning opportunities and sometimes you'll be the student and other times you'll be the teacher. In neither position should fear have ownership and control over you. It shouldn't keep you from seeking out new opportunities with the unknown fear of what could go wrong or the fear of judgement from others. Imagine what could go right. I've heard people say there's no such thing as a stupid question, yet it doesn't feel that way when you're the one asking the question. The judgement comes into play because people tend to remember your failures and mistakes and not so much your drive or success. We seldom give praise for just trying with disregard of the thought that it's not always easy to just show up and try.

We are all familiar with the phrase of "looking at the glass half full," meaning making a conscious decision to block the negative thoughts and only focus on the positive. Well, this isn't as easy for everyone and can be challenging for some. With that being said, it's not always the case that the person is negative, or a Debbie Downer as they say. It just well could be they struggle with anxiety. The mind is so powerful, and the bible tells us in Proverbs 23:7, *so a man thinketh so he is*. An anxious mind could be one of your biggest hurdles in life. Anxiety tied to fear should not prevent you from being the best version of yourself! Self-care is so much deeper than what's on the outside. We have to tend to our mental wellbeing also in order to reach that best version.

At some point in my life, it was clear that something was wrong. I often wondered why am I like this? This can't be normal, is it? How did I get this way? When and how did this all start? I can tell something is wrong with me I wonder can other people tell. I try to encourage myself and speak positive affirmations, but it only gets me so far. Do I even believe what I'm saying? How is it that my mind easily believes the negative thoughts but it's hard to believe or trust the positive ones. I've accomplished so much in the presence of my fears, yet I can't help but to wonder how much more I could've accomplished if I didn't allow my anxiety to have ownership over me. Where would I be had I not played it "safe and realistic." How much further I could've traveled down the road to success If I wouldn't have stopped at the caution signs and broken red lights I created in my mind. What if I had not made those U- turns out of fear of the unknown, and not allowed my anxiety to cripple me. How much more experienced, talented, successful, and confident I would be had I explored a little more, asked more questions, sought new opportunities to push myself to learn more, and admitted when I didn't understand.

Most importantly I should've spoken up in situations when I really wasn't okay. Not only during the pursuit of my education and career but also relationships, and life in general. Somehow, I programmed myself to just be quiet, suffer in silence and figure it out later privately. I feared being misunderstood or misjudged. I didn't want to make things worse for myself either, always convincing myself it's not so bad— I could handle it. If it's meant to be it will be. I created excuses to avoid conflict and justify what I was dealing with and feeling internally. In some situations, things could have been better, and I should've spoken up. So, again, I ask myself, how did I get like this? Where did this mindset come from? Where did it all start?

CHILDHOOD TRAUMAS

WERE YOU THE curious child without fear, creating adventures everywhere you went, or asking a thousand questions— inquisitive? Or were you the quiet, awkward child cautious and fearful of everything? Withdrawn to perhaps avoid drawing any attention to yourself? The poster child for "stay in a child's place" and "children should be seen not heard." At one point, I was both but at different times with each parent and depending on the environment.

With my father I was the curious adventurous child and with my mother I was the fearful, quiet one. I remember growing up feeling like I couldn't do anything right and all I did was make mistakes. I only felt like that with my mom. She constantly reminded me how imperfect I was and compared me to others such as my cousin and her friends' children. It felt like she was always so critical of everything about me. I was clumsy, shy, forgetful, overly sensitive, and

I took everything so personal. Well at least that's what I was told and how I felt.

I remember my dad called me and I got distracted like most kids do and I sat the phone down, and when I came back once I remembered he had hung up. I cried for hours because I had forgotten which caused him to hang up the phone and I was afraid that maybe he was mad at me. Now, most people would say just ask your mom to call him back. It wasn't that simple for me because I was too afraid of her. She was always so frustrated, and it scared me. I didn't like asking her for too much of anything! Not even as a young child. Yes, I guess I was pretty much a crybaby. I remember crying in private. I tried to hide for fear of embarrassment and making things worse. I would go find a hiding spot usually in my grandmother's closet, and cry because my feelings were always hurt. I cried whenever I had to leave my dad and go back to my mom. I cried whenever she yelled at me. I got teary eyed when she looked at me a certain way. I was so sensitive! Most kids you have to beat them in order for them to cry but for me, just look at me the wrong way with disappointment or any display of anger and it would just hurt my poor little feelings so bad. And like most mothers, any signs of tears she would yell "shut up before I give you something to cry about," so for that reason alone I would hide and cry in whatever safe space I could create. The self-isolation and silent tears led to struggles with loneliness, sadness, fear, disappointment, abandonment issues, and shame. I felt lonely because no one understood why I cried or why I was so sensitive. I didn't even understand. My dad: however, did allow me to be who I was, I didn't have to hide my emotions from him, and I never actually felt lonely in his presence. It's safe to say I shed less tears with him. I was a whole different child in his presence. The sadness and shame came from the disappointments. Ashamed that I was so sensitive and what most considered a "crybaby" around the age of seven and eight.

There was also a time when my mom was so overprotective and paranoid that it was embarrassing, confusing and shameful as well. She would physically check me on a regular basis to make sure no one had molested me. At the time, I thought it was normal and just what moms did to protect their daughters. As I got older and was able to go to the bathroom by myself and clean myself it started to feel abnormal. I never understood why she did this, and she never told me why. I suspected maybe something happened to her when she was my age. I'm not sure at what age she stopped checking me, but I do remember feeling the shame and embarrassment as time progressed like something was wrong with me that made her do that. I didn't understand why she would do that after I told her no one had touched me. It was very uncomfortable and began to feel like I was being punished and she never believed me. It felt like I did something wrong. I had a male cousin that was a few years older than me. One day while I was visiting my dad, he brought it up. I was about twelve years old, and he asked me, "Is your mom still acting crazed? Does she still check your private parts?" I had literally repressed that out of my memories and forgotten all about that. Then here he was reminding me, and I was so humiliated. It made me wonder how he even knew about that. Did he see her do it before or did he overhear family members talking about her. She would constantly ask me afterward, "Are you sure no one has touched you? Don't lie to me." Now as I got older, I understood she was just trying to protect me, but it didn't feel that way when I was younger. It was actually scary and traumatizing. The physical act of her checking my private parts felt so bad because she approached me hostile and usually angry. It seemed like I was in trouble instead of a mother protecting her child. I felt like she was interrogating me, and something was wrong with me. Even after I would tell her no one had touched me, she would call me a liar and tell me, "You know I don't like liars." I often wondered what happened to her to make her do that to me and why didn't she believe me.

It's obvious I struggled with my emotions as a young child. My mother could ask me a question and I would be scared to answer because it seemed like she never believed me, and everything was always my fault. I would try to process the question she was asking and find the right answer that wouldn't result in me getting yelled at. Sometimes she would try to trick me and see if I was really telling the truth or if I was lying to her. One day, she asked me something and I replied no then she said, "Well make something up and tell me." So, I did and then she said, "I knew you were lying." That was even more confusing for me. I had to be between the age of six and eight. The truth be told, if someone did touch me, I would have never told her because I was so afraid of her. I was always trying to gauge her emotions, so I knew how to proceed. My abandonment issues I felt resulted in low self-esteem, people pleasing, and so on. Looking back on my childhood, it's hard to understand how any child could have all these emotional issues at such a young age. Why was I so young and stressed out? It just wasn't normal! What happened that created and led to these overwhelming emotions? Was I born like this? Was this hereditary? I appeared "normal" or so I thought. I was always smiling and laughing, playing with other kids, slightly outgoing, and a smart "normal" student. I was in a gifted class in kindergarten. I remember being told how smart I was, how cute I looked, and how well my mom dressed me. She always kept my hair and appearance up. From the outside looking in everything appeared normal. I remember family and friends telling me how she wouldn't allow me to play like most kids because I couldn't get dirty. I had to always look cute and act cuter. After all, I was her first child and a reflection of her!

I was cute Monday through Friday and totally the opposite on the weekends. I was this prissy quiet shy girl with my mom and this talkative, sassy, adventurous tom boy with my dad. I spent every weekend at my great-grandmother's house where my father lived. I loved going over there, it was an outlet for me that I desperately needed. At Big Mama's house there were other family members that lived there as well, and I loved them all. It was always fun when it was a lot of people in the house. They had card parties on the weekends, my cousins would come over and sometimes spend the night. The house was just lively most of the time. Good energy, full of laughter! They would barbeque just because the weather was good, and I would play in the sprinklers during the summer like I was at a water park. It was my happy place. In some aspect it felt like the happiest moments of my childhood. I was able to be a kid.

I would go outside and play all day, sunup to sundown. I could ride my bike all through the neighborhood. I was able to go places with friends and cousins that I normally wouldn't have been allowed to go under my mom's supervision. My dad did odd jobs for the owner of the neighborhood candy store, Mr. Fitzgerald. He gave me a tab so I could get whatever I wanted with no money. At times, it felt like I was spoiled rotten, and I loved it! My dad gave me the freedom my mom didn't. He would let me do whatever I wanted, and my childhood felt great and somewhat normal for the most part. I was able to hang out with my friends and visit their homes. He even let me spend the night sometimes at the neighbor's house two houses down. This was huge because I couldn't do any of this with my mom. I was also able to hang out with my cousins and go places with them. Once it got dark, I had to stay in front of the house and on the porch. Some nights I would be out to one in the morning, in the yard catching lightening bugs in a jar, watching the older kids hang out, and all the action on the block. Weekends and summertime in the Chi were great with my dad! It represented everything I couldn't do with my mom. My Big mama, along with my dad, gave me that outlet to just be a kid and I enjoyed it. They always cooked; I had hot breakfast every morning. My dad made me lunch, usually a sandwich and he would cut the crust off and cut them in fours or triangles with a pickle, chips, and a juice. Big Mama cooked dinner every evening and I had all the snacks a kid could want. I watched "Wheel of Fortune" some evenings with Big Mama and other evenings I played cards with my daddy. My dad made me a swing hanging from the tree in the backyard and we built playhouses out of boxes and forts in the living room with chairs and blankets. I watched the soap operas with Big Mama some days and her favorite was *Young and Restless*. We went grocery shopping, to the bank, and to visit her boyfriend in Maywood at the time. I remember going to bingo some evenings with her and her friends with a bunch of change in a Crown Royal bag. We would also get on the train, which was down the street from the house and ride it to the end of the line and just come back. She called it people watching. I remember going to girl scout meetings with my friend that stayed two houses down and to her cheerleading practices. I did things I wanted to do or would've liked to do but didn't have the opportunity with my mom. And let's not forget the block clubs every year at the end of the summer! I always felt so much love from over there. I could be myself, didn't have to be perfect. I wasn't afraid to say I was hungry or anything I was feeling. I felt free on the weekends.

Living with my mom was totally the opposite. I felt like a prisoner, and I had to be perfect or appear to be, but I was far from it. It seemed as though I was always saying or doing the wrong thing. Thinking back, it just felt like my mom was always angry, frustrated, and on edge which made me on edge and nervous around her. I tried my best to stay out of her way and not get on her nerves. You know how they say kids should be seen and not heard. I wasn't trying to do either! By the way, now I know how unhealthy that way of thinking is. My mom was always like a ticking time bomb waiting to explode. I kind of knew what would set her off but never knew when she would go off and to what degree. This is why kids wait until their parents get on the phone gossiping to ask for anything. She was in a good mood gossiping on the phone with her friend, trying to spill the tea laughing and that was the perfect time to strike! Mom, I'm hungry? She would brush me off and say go get a snack. Mom, can I have money for the book fair this week? Go get my purse. More than likely, she agreed to anything to get me out of her face. I learned really quickly to start seizing my moments of opportunity whenever she was distracted and in a good mood! However, just imagine the joy I had when Friday came along! My Big mama would pick me up from school, she would take me to White Castle or Long

John Silver's to get me some hush puppies before heading to my weekend home.

In my mind, my mom provided a place to live and clothes to wear, which was extremely important but at that age of course I didn't see it that way. She was the strict parent that didn't play any games and she was the authoritarian. My dad, on the other hand, was my best friend. He gave me love, and attention and cavities from all the junk food I had on credit. He made me feel perfect like absolutely nothing was wrong with me. Yes, I was a daddy's girl. He provided an environment that I felt I could thrive in as a child, compared to living with my mom it felt like a safe place that allowed me to just be me. Vulnerable when I needed to be and free to express all my emotions at any time.

However, Dad was not perfect; he had his own set of issues that I was fully aware of, but it didn't matter at that age. He still provided the love and attention that I craved and needed. He was a semi-functioning drug addict that took care of his daughter on the weekends. But I wouldn't consider him just a weekend dad. My dad was probably the only man my mom ever trusted back then. Not only did he have me on the weekends, but once my mother had another child and she got potty trained, he started keeping her also. Me and my sister are six years apart and obviously we have different fathers. My dad also became her dad, and he would keep us during the week if Mom had something to do. My dad and her dad became friends, and he would come over my great-grandmother's house sometimes and see us. They were two dads with their two daughters creating the village that was very much needed.

He did little odd jobs for several people around the neighborhood. I remember collecting aluminum cans with him and taking them to the recycling center and then he would take me and my sister to spend the money. He would fix things for people, wash their cars, and cut their grass. We did so much walking then, and what would be embarrassing now but then I enjoyed every moment of it! I just wanted to be with him no matter what or where we were going.

Although that was my happy place, growing up with a drug addict as a father definitely had its downside. We used to go to Handy Andy store, which was huge sort of like a Menards. He would steal small things like flashlights, lighters, little tool sets stuff he could fit in his pocket. He would then return the stuff later for store credit and either buy something he could sell on the street or get me something like candy or a toy for my sister and me. He did get caught once when I was with him, and my grandmother had to come get me. Sometimes my dad would try to sell my sister's dad some of the stolen items even though he didn't need them. He was a truck driver and money was never an issue, but he would actually buy the items just to put some money in my dad's pocket. There were also times he just gave him money just because. Of course, my mom never found out about any of this either.

Every year he bought me a new bike and then turned around and sold it. He even sold a few of my puppies or somehow, they just ran away, according to him. I had an all-black poodle name Fuji, a baby pit, and a German Shepard. He sold every last one of them. He never did admit to how each one eventually came up missing. It wasn't just my things he sold either; he had gotten so bad that he would sell my grandmother's meat out of her freezer and take money out of her purse. I felt so bad for my Big mama. He was driving her crazy. None the less, I was still a daddy's girl. He always made up for it later somehow.

I'll never forget how he took my school fundraiser papers around the neighborhood selling candy for me. What a great father right! I just knew I was going to win the biggest prize they had available! Well, it was all a scam. He kept all those people's money, and I was so embarrassed. My big mama had to do damage control a lot to try to keep the peace amongst her neighbors. At this point, everyone in the neighborhood knew he was on drugs. Although he had one of those personalities where people just loved him regardless of his addiction, they knew he couldn't be trusted. My mom said he was a loving con artist.

I did have some scary moments with my dad on those adventures as I called them. I would usually go with him to buy drugs because he just couldn't say no to me, and I wanted to follow him everywhere he went. I was fearful at times that something would happen to him while I was with him. Not sure what I could have done, but I wanted to protect my daddy as well. I figured he was safer because he had a child with him. Back then, there was a little respect for women and children. I thought who would hurt him while he had his daughter with him. He probably thought the same thing. Being a parent myself, I really can't believe this man took his daughter with him to buy drugs. Of course, my mother never knew anything about this as well, plus I would've never told her in fear of not being able to see my daddy again.

There is this one memory that has stuck with me my entire life. It was during my weekend stay and it was dark outside. We walked a few blocks to what I thought were the projects. We walked into the hallway of one of the buildings. It was cold, dirty, and smelled. There were a couple of young men that looked extremely scary to me. They were shooting dice, drinking, and smoking. Now, I knew they drug dealers; I wasn't naive. Also, I learned about the D.A.R.E program at school, so I somewhat knew about drugs. He started talking to one of the boys while the others looked at me all crazy as I tried not to make eye contact. They exchanged words and then he gave him some money. The guy then proceeded to use his hand to push the tile up slightly as he reached up to get something out of the ceiling and gave it to my dad and then we left. As we walked back home, I didn't ask any questions because I already knew what had just happened. I also knew the routine. We would get back home go upstairs to the attic where we stayed and he would get his small mirror the size of a plate, a razor, lighter and his pipe. He would tell me to go play with my toys because he didn't want me to see him do the drugs. Of course, I never listened, and it wasn't like he would put me out, so I saw everything. These "adventures" became normal for me. Thank God at that time, during the 1980's, drug dealers had some type of moral decency about them. They cared about children, older people, and women. Can you imagine in this day and age how many things could have gone wrong? That memory was what later led to me having constant nightmares of someone killing my dad in front of me or me finding him dead with a sheet over his body.

For years well into my thirties I would have nightmares that took place at my big mama's house. It was always a group of men breaking in through the back door while I was there alone, and I would run and hide in the basement or attic, then tried to escape out the front door or the basement door that led to the back door. Now the front door had a key that big mama used to lock it from the inside. In my dreams, I would try to find the key that was usually kept in a cabinet by the door and fumbled to unlock the door to run to the neighbor's house that I used to spend the night at. Even though it was several people that lived at my big mama's home, I was always alone in the dream. I mean constantly having the same dream over and over twenty years plus. Each time I would jump up out of my sleep and try to stay awake long enough, so the dream didn't continue when I fell back to sleep. It was so disturbing to the point I started asking myself what happened in that house?

I came to realize that maybe all those years it was the fear of what I thought could've happened that was haunting me. My dad's addiction, along with other factors, was what led to my grandmother moving back to Birmingham, Alabama. Of course, my dad didn't have anywhere to go so he just followed her there. That was a huge transition for both of us. I cried for a long time behind them leaving me in Chicago alone. I was probably around the age of ten or eleven when they left. It broke my heart!

THE RECOVERY

THE YEARS AFTER my dad and my grandmother left Chicago were extremely difficult. I had no place to go on the weekends, which meant I had no outlet from what felt like pure hell. I was forced to be with my mother every single day and that was a huge deal for me. My happy place didn't exist anymore or our dysfunctional adventures. I eventually adjusted like all changes in life. During this time, my sister's dad kind of took over for him as much as he could as well. He would pick us up and take us to the movies, out to eat, or to Toys R' Us. He would then drop us off and give us five or ten dollars to split. As you know, he was a truck driver, and we would play inside the truck whenever he was in town. As kids, we were so fascinated that he had a bed and a TV inside the truck. We thought it was the coolest thing ever.

While my father was in Birmingham, he eventually got clean and left the drugs alone. It wasn't overnight though; it took several tries with him in and out of rehabs. My younger sister and I started spending our summers down south in

Alabama and each year my father seemed to get healthier and better. He was working a steady job, contributing to the household, and helping financially with me and my sister, which was something I never saw him do before. He started helping my mom financially; he bought school clothes for the first time. He bought me my first pair of eyeglasses. I had been telling my mom that I had problems with my vision; however, she never believed me. She thought I was just saying it for attention because I had a friend that wore glasses. That first summer down there, he bought me two pairs of glasses and I was so proud and happy. Afterwards, he took me and my sister to the zoo and one of my lenses fell out. Go figure. They were cheap but good thing I had an extra pair. To my mom's surprise, yes, I was really blind, and I've been wearing glasses ever since. Do you think she ever admitted she was wrong? Of course not. He would take us to the park, the mall, and we went to the dollar store at least twice a week. We thought he had so much money because we spent it all. There was no way he could even support a drug habit with me and my little sister there. By this time, I was around thirteen and my sister was seven. I was into shopping, and she was always hungry and wanted toys.

With this new father I had, he was addressing all of his baby girl's issues. For years I had been suffering with stomach problems and my mom nor my dad took me to the doctor for it. He was always my doctor. I remember my dad giving me Pepto Bismol and rubbing my stomach while I was in pain until I would fall asleep. I had drunk so much of that stuff when I was younger it was like juice to me. Now that he had health insurance, he took me to the doctor while I was there, and the doctor informed us that I had a hernia, which we knew already because it was visible. So that summer, not sure if it was the same summer or the next, I had surgery to remove the hernia. Unfortunately, the pain didn't stop. It only eased up slightly, so he took me right back to the doctor. I'll never forget the doctor saying that everything was normal, and they couldn't find anything else wrong with me. Final diagnosis was, "she has a nervous stomach."

Once my dad left Chicago, he pretty much vowed to never come back again. I believe it was because he was afraid of falling back into that lifestyle of addiction. He struggled for so long trying to get clean and stay clean. Even when they first moved back to the south, he had so many relapses. It wasn't until May of 1999 that he returned for my high school graduation. He was so proud of me, but I was prouder of him and who he had become. Him and my grandmother stayed a couple of days and we celebrated with family and friends. Somehow it was a graduation and a family reunion all in one. We had family from New York, Pennsylvania, and Birmingham. So, ghetto lol. Whatever it was, it was nice and one of my fondest pre-adult memories.

That summer when I went to visit him, he bought me my first car. It was a 1989 Ford Tempo that he financed making biweekly payments. I think back myself and ask what we were thinking! Well, I know what I was thinking. I just wanted a car— any car. Although he was working and doing well, he really couldn't even afford it, no matter how old it was. I don't even think he knew what credit really was, but he got it anyway. During the process, we went to the dealership, and they asked me what I planned on doing with my car. I would respond and say take it back to Chicago where I live. Then my dad told me to stop telling them that because it's keeping them from approving him. He further explained they thought I wasn't going to keep up with the payments and they wouldn't be able to find the car. Well, that's exactly what eventually happened.

He drove it back to Chicago after the summer and flew back to Alabama the next day. He was determined to make up for the years of my childhood during his addiction when he was unable to provide for me the way he would have liked to. Little did he know, although my childhood wasn't perfect most of my best memories were with him. As abnormal as my childhood was, it felt normal to me at the time.

DEAR MAMA

THE ONLY PERSON I loved, admired, respected, yet feared and resented at times was my dear mother. I misunderstood the woman she was and the level of pain she carried around that was deeply rooted in childhood trauma as well. We had a complicated relationship that I hid from her the majority of my life, even as an adult. I couldn't dare tell her what and how she made me feel! I was scared. Scared that she wouldn't understand, she wouldn't care, or she would just be angry at me. I was her first born. She had me at nineteen-years-old and I had my daughter at nineteen as well. My mom was my sole provider of all material things. She provided a place to live, clothes to wear, shoes on my feet, and took care of me. She cooked sometimes. Christmas was always awesome she went above and beyond every year! She made dreams come true!! But it was always something missing that I desperately needed and wanted from my mother. I always knew my mother loved me, and I loved her, but it felt like a complicated kind of love.

Honestly, there were times it didn't feel unconditional. Yes, she loved me and took care of me, but I wasn't sure she liked me. I'm not talking about those hard teenage years either. By then the damage was already done and the resentment was already stewing. It felt like she just tolerated being my mother because she had no choice and who else was going to do it. My father was a drug addict that couldn't support himself let alone a child. As much as I loved my father, I realized he could've never been the full-time custodial parent! Hell, if she wasn't expecting me home Sunday evenings or Monday mornings, he might have sold me too. I'm sure that wouldn't have actually happened because he was also afraid of her.

She was a tough woman and didn't take any mess from anybody. She was headstrong and tough as nails. Not an ounce of weakness anywhere. She only stood five feet tall and had a personality twice her size and not an ounce of fear within her, at least that's what she wanted people to think. Here I was totally the opposite. This overly sensitive child that longed for affection, acceptance, and constant reassurance that I was good enough. Good enough to be her daughter, good enough even though I was clumsy, forgetful, and awkward. Good enough to be accepted as not perfect but imperfect and know that it's okay. Okay to be sensitive. I wanted so badly for her to just acknowledge my feelings and say I'm sorry I hurt you. Yes, your feelings matter Shanta even as a child. I wanted to feel safe with her!

Sometimes we don't realize how our children need more

hugs and verbal expressions of love. Not only do children want to feel loved, but they need that security blanket to feel safe as well. There needed to be a healthy balance of discipline as well as physical acts of love and security. As a small child, I don't remember getting that from my mother. I do remember getting it from my father. I felt his unconditional love no matter what was going on. There aren't childhood memories of my mom hugging me, kissing me, wiping my tears, telling me she loved me, holding me while I was sick, or comforting me when I needed it. I'm sure some of it may have happened but I just don't have those memories. It makes me question do they actually exist? I do have a few as an adult with her. Everyone talks about daddy's girl and mama's boy, not realizing that mother-daughter relationships are very much crucial and very much needed. I literally came from her, yet I felt so disconnected from her. That mother-daughter relationship teaches you how to become a woman and how to love and nurture. I believe as a daughter we get our strength from our mothers.

I think over the years and as my mom began to have more kids, she changed, and she softened up a lot. Maybe she matured as well. During my childhood, it was like she was so hardcore all the time. Maybe she felt like she had to be that way. I also believe it made a huge difference that my mother eventually married. My younger sisters having their father in the home took a lot of the burden off my mother, which made a big difference. She became emotionally available for them. I noticed the difference in the mother me and Kia had and the mother they were getting. She was no longer operating in survival mode. Prior to that, she was really doing it on her own. As a young child before then I remember never wanting to be at home with her and crying hysterically when my dad and Big Mama would drop me off and leave me. Later in life, she told me how much it used to hurt her, and how she could never understand why I never wanted to be with her.

As a mother myself I can imagine the hurt she felt from that, which is why I hid my feelings from her as long as I did. Also, I couldn't bare hurting anyone's feelings, especially my mom. It's not like she was this horrible mother and physically abusive. I just felt like she was so emotionally detached or unavailable, and for whatever reason I was just an emotional child.

My mother was a young, strong, independent hard-working single mother, doing the best she knew how while raising two daughters six years apart. For the longest, I remember it being just the three of us. The three of us sleeping in a queen-sized bed in a one-bedroom apartment. Prior to that, there was a time when we lived with my grandmother who I loved like crazy, and I was her favorite by the way. Just like my big mama's house, there were a lot of people in that home as well, but it wasn't as fun. I actually hated it there. Don't get me wrong, kids came over when they partied, and my grandmother cooked some great meals for everyone! However, it still wasn't the same. It was actually overcrowded and depressing. One house represented peace and the other was chaotic! Now that I think about it, it was probably chaotic for my mother as well. Especially being the only girl with three brothers.

The older I became, the more our relationship became complicated. I began to really resent her as I became more anxious, intimidated, and self-conscious! Welcome to the pre-teen and teenage years!! Later, after moving back from Harrisburg, Pennsylvania, we moved in with my grandmother again once I entered high school. This was even worse because it was smaller, less space, and on the third floor. However, we were only there temporarily while her and my stepdad looked for a house. Well, one evening my male cousin was there like every weekend; however, this evening it was just us at home. We were watching TV and my mother came home from work and rang the doorbell. I'm not sure why she didn't have a key. Anyways, we were arguing over who was going to go open the door because we were on the third floor. He was persistent and said, "It's your mom, so you open the door." So, I did. When she came upstairs and realized it was just us there, I was interrogated for at least a week about it.

According to her, I took so long to open the door because we were doing something we had no business doing. As I pleaded with her that I was a virgin and that's not something I would ever do, she made it known that I was a liar and nasty. That hurt me so bad she thought I would even do something like that. Of course, at this point I was too old for her to physically check me, so she made sure to make me feel worthless and like a liar. She never even said anything to him about it, just me. I was so disgusted I told my Grandmother Dot, which is her mom. She told me not to worry about it. She reiterated that everyone knows how unstable my mom could be and not to let her negativity get to me.

We eventually ended up moving into our new home in Bellwood, which I loved! By the time I reached my junior year I was ready to move out. Although we had this new, spacious home with just us, things became worse between us. It seemed like I was always being attacked and nothing I did was ever good enough. I tried my best to stay out of her way and not to make her angry. I was never the rebellious teen that talked back and was disobedient— that was actually Kia. I mean, I definitely wasn't perfect, and I did some wrong, but it was minimal. She did a great job of instilling that fear in me. The problem with that "method" is you're afraid to speak up and you learn to suppress all your emotions out of fear. You become anxious questioning what could go wrong and possibly make think worse, fearing the judgment of other's reaction. Just overthinking everything. Questioning will your behavior or words cause them not to love you anymore, like you, or respect you. Then you start to question if your emotions are valid? *Maybe it's something wrong with me that I feel this way. Maybe I'm being too sensitive or overreacting.* Then you convince yourself that expressing your emotions is seen as a sign of weakness and once people think you are weak; they try to take advantage of you. I can only speak from my own experience, but that fear stayed with me a long time and I took it everywhere I went.

All my life I was told I was so well behaved, quiet, timid, and shy. Fear will make you afraid to rock the boat and accept whatever is in front of you. It can cause you not to ask questions or at least the ones you're afraid to know the answers to. Fear can cause you to always play it safe and never challenge authority. You avoid conflict at all costs, even sacrificing your own peace and comfort. You miss opportunities because of fear! God forbid it's something seriously wrong and I should speak up. I would rather suffer in silence and deal with the consequences on my own. It won't kill me! That's the saying right? What doesn't kill you only makes you stronger! In a sense they lied!!! It may not kill you, but it definitely can break you and your mental health becomes compromised.

During my teenage years into my young adult years our relationship was unbearable at times; however, I would never really show it. I was the oldest of four girls now and I spent the majority of my teens caring for my siblings while my mom worked and also went out with her friends. At that time, I really didn't care I was glad she was gone. My teenage years literally sucked!! I had a few close friends that my mother knew very well so she did let up some but not much. The crazy part about it is, they loved her! She was funny, told it like it was, and spared no feelings!

I remember asking permission to leave my junior year in high school. I hated my school. I was physically struggling in school, emotionally struggling at home, and mentally breaking down. I just wanted and needed to get away. The plan was to move to Alabama with my father. He had sent me money for a Greyhound ticket. I packed up my clothes and my boyfriend came to pick me up, but she wouldn't allow me to leave. She told me there was no running away from my problems and I had to deal with it. Well, she was right and I'm so grateful she made me stay. I really didn't want to leave my boyfriend anyway, but I would've left had she let me. I believe she really made me stay to be her babysitter. Kids now- a-days just run away but I was too scared to do that! My mother worked for the airlines; she would have been on a flight so fast. She would have been waiting at the Greyhound station in Alabama ready to take me right back! And if you know her then you know there wouldn't have been no conversation had just hands thrown!! My grandmother in Alabama knew how I felt and she understood, and she told me, "Shanta, just do whatever you have to do to keep the peace in the house." I thought I was doing that already, but I made some adjustments. I stopped complaining to my dad because that only made things worse for me. Before I would complain to him and then he would call her and of course I would get cursed out along with him and things would be even worse. Her words and tone carried power!!

I stopped ditching school, which she never knew about anyways and gave it my all. I tried to help more around the house. I started staying after school for tutoring, which worked out because that meant I didn't have to be at home as much. My mother didn't allow me to work she said school was my only job, so I studied more, I braided hair on the weekends to make money, and my dad sent me and my sister, Kia, money and care packages as well. He had been doing that for me and Kia since he moved.

When senior year came, things were a little better. I had a little more freedom. My siblings were older, she didn't depend on me as much, and also I think she felt like I had earned it. This allowed me to have an outlet for what felt like my misery, which was my boyfriend and his family. Then I graduated.

Life was better as a young adult. I was fresh out of high school in a three-year relationship. I started attending a community college, working hard to get into the nursing program. I was finally able to work and earn my own money and I had a car also thanks to my dad. I was able to spend more time with my boyfriend and his family who I absolutely adored. They seem so close and normal. They spent time with each other, took vacations together, and had Sunday dinners that I loved! They also welcomed me and made me feel a part of their family. So, it wasn't soon after I ended up pregnant at eighteen.

Like any mother, mine was disappointed and upset! Rightfully so! She always told me no matter what you do, you better not bring any babies in my house so if you get pregnant be prepared to find you somewhere to live! I thought that meant while I was in high school. So, I remained a virgin until I graduated high school and boom pregnant first-time having sex. I'll never forget my Grandmother Dot said, "Well you knew she was going to have sex sooner or later." Grandma Dot was the only person that could check my mother and was not afraid of her! My mom of course, trying to maintain that hardcore exterior attitude, wasn't having it. She meant what she said and said what she meant. I dare you disobey me!! So that meant get out of my house and take Kia with me, who happened to be twelve at the time. I cannot remember what she did, but she has a story of her own, so I'll just focus on mine. Maybe it was the fact that she was my sidekick that I had to take everywhere I went and somehow, I still got pregnant. I'm not sure what it really was that she had done; however, we both were told to leave. My little sister went to live with her grandmother on her dad's side and I went to my boyfriend mother's house. It didn't last long; I was back home the same day. My stepdad called and said, "Your mom is mad, you need to help more around the house and come home." Somehow, I was the only one that got that call. But thank God for my stepdaddy! He literally made life more bearable when he came along for all of us! I always said the day he married my mother God wrote his name in the book of life and gave him a permanent seat in Heaven! God bless him!!!

After coming back home it took my mom some time to adjust to the fact that I was pregnant and having a child of my own. My boyfriend wasn't allowed over for a while because she said she needed time before she could look at him again. Once she decided enough time had passed, she allowed him to come back over. To reacclimate him, she decided to chase him around the house with a machete to instill a little fear in him. Afterward, she was ok with it and secretly became ready to become a grandmother. She would have never hurt him, but she obviously enjoyed putting fear into people and found it amusing.

She refused to attend the baby shower my boyfriend's mom threw for us. Instead, she made me take my younger sisters. I'm sure that was so they could come back and tell her everything. I can't tell you about the negative stuff without telling the positive as well. Aside from my childhood issues, she stood by me after that initial shock wore off. She supported me and loved me in spite of my life changing decision. I was a young, new mother just like herself at one time. Maybe she remembered what that felt like for her.

She drove me to the hospital when I went into labor. She cursed out the nurse after she compared walking with me through the hallways to walking her dog. She was coaching me with my breathing and then she called my boyfriend and said, "Get here now!" She was excited! I remember her telling me I was going to be in labor for hours, if not at least a day. She left to run home to get her camcorder, thinking she was going to record her baby giving birth! Thankfully, God had other plans. Jaelyn was born right after she left.

When she came back, she was so shocked. I remember her saying, "Don't think it's this easy all the time, you got lucky! You better not get pregnant in my house again." None the less she was secretly happy, excited, and proud. Her first granddaughter and she named her Jaelyn Samone. Yes, she was the one to name her. I couldn't dare take that away from her. Granny is what she called her. They had a beautiful bond from the beginning!

INADEQUACY

HAVE YOU EVER felt like you carry the weight of the world on your shoulders and everything that happens to or around you seem to be magnified to a greater height? You're trying so desperately to hold on, keep it all together, appear normal, feel normal and just survive. Inadequacy is the inability to deal with a situation or with life. I was once a sweet, timid, fearful, sensitive, easy going go with the flow kind of girl. In order to function daily and hold on to every bit of my sanity, I had to develop tough skin. I had to be able to shake some things off or try to convince others and myself I could shake it off. In the process I became bitter, angry, short tempered, impatient, anxious, and an overthinker. I was still sensitive, but I hid it more, so it wasn't so easily noticeable by others. I also adapted new ways to handle my sensitivity instead of crying so much.

Aside from overthinking by over analyzing every situation, conversation, and deep thought; I began to guard my heart. I appeared cold at times and nonchalant all while internalizing my emotions to the point I became this highly anxious person. I learned to suppress my emotions at least the ones that I felt made me look and feel weak. I didn't want to be that sensitive little girl anymore. I was tired of being hurt, emotionally vulnerable, and crying in private. I was tired of feeling period! I learned how to turn my love for people off when it no longer benefited me. I refused to allow anyone's lack of love or disrespect to damage me any more than I already was. After all, I was used to suffering in silence and feeling alone anyway. I learned to become an emotionally detached version of my mother.

My mother used to tease me or warn me about how mental illness ran in my family on my father's side. My grandmother had a nervous condition and suffered from panic attacks, depression, and anxiety. My uncle was schizophrenic. My grandmother had been medicated and under the care of a psychiatrist since her early twenties. My father started having panic attacks later in life and he battled depression as well. They were so severe he struggled with small tasks such as going to the grocery store. It became so overwhelming that one day he had to leave everything and just run out and that was the last time he ever attempted grocery shopping. A man that at one time could not stay still and loved taking his dogs to the park, going to Church's Chicken, the mall, and McDonald's a few times a week and loved grocery shopping, couldn't handle leaving the house. When he told me this, I asked him why he wouldn't just seek help. Like most people he didn't believe in therapy and was against medication as well. He replied, "I took enough drugs in my lifetime." I tried to convince him this was different, but he wasn't hearing me. I believe he was afraid of addiction. He always said that he'll always be an addict no matter how long he's been clean.

Everyone goes through heartbreak, depression, and anxiety at some point. When does it become a problem and considered a form of mental illness? According to American Psychiatric Association, *nearly one in five (19%) U.S. adults experience some form of mental illness.* The Mayo Clinic describes mental health disorders as a wide range of mental health conditions affecting your mood, thinking, and behavior. Anxiety disorders are more frequent in women than men, they usually present themselves during childhood and adolescence, 50-80% of the cases coexist with other anxiety disorders, mood disorders, and substance use disorders (Roberge et al.,2022). The Global Burden of Disease Study ranks anxiety disorders as the sixth leading cause of years of life lived with disability (2022).

Ever since I was a child, I've felt different, inadequate at times, just a roller coaster of emotions. Everything seems to affect me so deeply. Often times, things and situations that really don't fully concern me. It's like I absorb other people's problems, their fears, pain, worry, and disappointment, which is why I'm very selective about the company I keep and my environment. Why can't I control my thoughts, which leads to the anxiety. I had no idea why I was like this. I'm pretty sure this is how I became a people pleaser and what I call a fixer upper. I'm always trying to fix someone and make them better, always asking myself how I can be of service and help those who are in need? Maybe somehow fixing other people distracts me from my own problems and insecurities. Maybe I know what it feels like to want someone to care enough about your struggles and needs that they extend a helping hand without judgement.

When I was in elementary school, I started writing poetry. It was a way to express my emotions freely and safely. I remember my first contest when I won a hundred dollars. I was in fourth or fifth grade and Gwendolyn Brooks came to my school. She was an African American poet and author. She held a poetry contest and of course I entered. It didn't require me to do anything but submit a poem. I didn't have to read it, be seen, or anything, so I did. I was in complete shock when I actually won! I believe there were a few winners not just me; however, I was extremely proud of myself. I didn't enter the contest to win; I just wanted someone to read my thoughts and words. That was the beginning of me creating a healthy and positive way to release my emotions. It was easier to write than it was to speak.

I remember entering a few more contests through the years and presenting at my grandfather's church in Alabama a few times. I also entered a contest one summer while I was there. I saw the contest listed in a magazine and decided to go for it. My love for writing was growing stronger and stronger. That summer I was informed via mail by the publishers of a book that was affiliated with the contest that my writing was selected to appear in a section of their book along with other contestants that entered the contest as well. The catch was they also tried to get you to purchase the book, which of course no one in my family did so I never received confirmation if my work was published. What I did receive was the inspiration I needed to keep writing, keep expressing my emotions and thoughts through words and paper even if I could never possess the courage to actually speak them.

During this time, I kept my poetry and writings in a notebook. I managed to hold on to it all the way through my sophomore year in high school until the day I lost it. I had no recollection of what happened to it I just knew it was gone forever. The thought of someone finding my notebook and reading all my personal feelings and fears was devastating. After that, I stopped writing. I managed to hide it from my mother all that time to lose it and be read by a stranger. The great escape was over and I was left with nothing but my anxious thoughts proceeding like nothing happened.

APPREHENSIVE

MY FIRST PHYSICAL encounter with anxiety that I was aware of was when I was in respiratory school. During my first year in the program, my mom was diagnosed with breast cancer, and I remember sitting in the waiting room with my stepdad studying while she was having a mastectomy. That was in 2008 and afterward, she had a fairly good recovery, was in remission and it seemed like life went back to normal. That first year was stressful but the real struggle came that second year, which was around 2010.

I worked so hard and pushed myself in ways I never imagined or thought I was capable of. I gave up my perfect full-time schedule to go part-time, which was technically thirty hours a week and struggle financially even more. I was alternating working second shift 3-11p.m. and night shift 11-7 p.m. while going to school full time, having to go to clinicals, and being a mom. For two years I spent many nights falling asleep at my kitchen table, studying and drinking energy drinks.

I remember trying to take caffeine pills one night before a big exam so I could stay up and study. Well things didn't go as planned because I ended up in the ER getting pumped with fluids and missed the exam. The ER doctor told me so kindly, "Throw that mess away and don't let me see you for this nonsense again! I'll give you a note and hopefully you can take your exam when you return." It wasn't until one day I was in clinicals, and I couldn't stop shaking. This was the last semester and my final clinical site. I had to give a presentation and I was so nervous my voice, hands, and knees were shaking uncontrollably. I was sweating like I was standing in a sauna. Now, our uniform included hunter green scrubs and a long white lab coat that came past my knees because I'm so short, which I was so thankful for that day. It kind of hid my shaky knees. I had never experienced that type of fear before. That was the first and beginning of me not having control over my body. Now, I only had to give the presentation to my preceptor who was also the manager. I was extremely intimidated by him and due to my overthinking; I convinced myself in my head that I should give the presentation to a room full of doctors and residents first and get past my nerves so then when I give the presentation to him, I wouldn't be as nervous. I know it sounds ridiculous, but this was my anxious logical thinking at the time. If I knew then what I know now about the relationship/rapport between doctors and respiratory therapist, I wouldn't have embarrassed myself like that. They told me that day, "For future purposes you know you don't diagnosis anyone right." I responded, "Yes I know this was just for classroom purposes and I was forced to do so." Also, it didn't work presenting to a room full of doctors was useless, I was just as nervous when I presented to him. So, I ended up presenting it twice and suffered both times instead of one.

I wish the lack of logic and anxious reckless behavior stopped there. Unfortunately, not! Let me tell you how I damaged my car going to clinicals one morning because I was running late and extremely nervous. I was getting in the turning lane and somehow I was too close to this semi-truck and something on the back of it grabbed my mirror and I scraped my car from the front to the back. It literally looked like Wolverine or Edward Scissor Hands had keyed my car. You know what I did? Kept going until I made it to my clinicals and then I accessed the damage. Yes, I had damaged the whole passenger's side of my car rushing to get to my unpaid clinicals on time and was still late, and nobody actually cared but me. I wasn't the only one late either. My preceptor was late as well! We pulled up at the same time and he asked me what happened to my car, and I told him. He responded it's never that serious, look at me we're both late. I thought to myself what is wrong with me?? Why am I like this?? Why do I torture myself like this? Thank goodness my stepdad had a cousin that did bodywork. Sad to say, but he got a lot of business from me down the line. Anyways, only by the grace of God I was able to make it through that program.

Two months before my graduation from the RT

program, I received a call from the manager at my clinical site I had to give that awful presentation at. He offered me a position there once I graduated. This was my worst clinical rotation because the manager seemed so hard on me, which was why I was so intimated and nervous about my presentation. He interrogated and quizzed me daily about everything. He would call me and my classmate into his office at the end of the day and ask, "So what did you learn today?" My brain did not work like that. My nerves seem to paralyze me and suddenly, I cannot remember anything besides what I ate for lunch unless I wrote it down. He would proceed to ask a bunch of clinical questions that I rarely answered correctly, even though I knew the answer. So, imagine to my surprise when he called and said, "I know you're about to graduate soon, and I would love for you to come work here." I was so excited I couldn't believe it; I had secured a job before I even graduated and taken my state boards. He told me what day to come in to meet with him to discuss everything.

When the day finally arrived, I made sure to dress professionally. I had my resume and references available, ready in hand. I walked into his office excited and confident. I was immediately greeted by him and the director of nursing. It was an interview, and I was not prepared! Completely my fault because if you stay ready then you don't have to get ready. But at that time, I felt blindsided. I was so confused because he called me. I never applied for a job or inquired about one either. Truth be told, I was so intimidated by him that I had no desire to even work there. Well, that was the worst interview of my life! They asked me clinical questions that I should have known, and I did know; however, I wasn't mentally prepared, my anxiety got the best of me, I got extremely nervous, and bombed the interview. Of course, I didn't get the job and I was devastated. The little confidence I had was destroyed.

When it came time to take my exit exam in school, I felt so discouraged that I called my grandfather who was a pastor and I asked him to pray over me. Well, Grandaddy Rufus asked me what was going on and I told him. He prayed with me over the phone, and it went something like this, "Lord whatever your will is, let it be done." I thought to myself really. *That's all you got. What about the blood and asking God to give me wisdom and knowledge?* Well, I guess it was enough because May rolled around, and I graduated! I waited until December of that year to take my CRT exam to become a Certified Respiratory Therapist and waited until February of 2012 to take my RRT exam to become a Registered Respiratory Therapist.

My anxiety was still very much present and had taken a front row seat during that time. I made it a priority to practice my interviewing skills, covering clinical as well as common interview questions. I did research and printed out pages of common interview questions and created answers for every last one of them. I continued to study my respiratory notes so that I wouldn't forget anything. I finally landed my first job around May of 2012.

I still can't believe even now with over ten years' experience under my belt I still have days I struggle with my nerves and doubt my own capabilities. Considering how bad my anxiety had gotten, somedays it would be a struggle just trying to hold a pen and write on my assignment sheet. I started shaking whenever I attempted a simple task such as checking a patient's pulse. It was like anything that I tried to do with my hands would trigger me to think about my movement first and my tremors would automatically start. It was like I was having performance anxiety. Even something that required nothing and meant to be relaxing such as getting my nails done became a problem. If I'm distracted, I'm fine but if I focus on the person touching my hand I start shaking. It started to bother me so bad because the nail tech would tell me to be still and I couldn't, so I stopped getting my nails done for about a year or so.

HORNEY

KAREN HORNEY WAS a German psychoanalyst. I personally identified with her logic and personality theory. I discovered Karen Horney while pursuing my bachelor's degree in psychology. Her theories helped me to make sense of what I had already known about myself and my childhood. Karen Horney described her relationship with her father as intimidation, sternness, and a demanding manner, which I related to with my mother. According to the textbook, "Theories of Personality," Horney's personality theory describes how a lack of love in childhood fosters anxiety and hostility. Horney agreed with Freud that early childhood years shaped the adult's personality. Instead of biological forces, the social relationship between children and their parents is the key factor.

Horney believed childhood was dominated by the safety need— a higher-level need for security and freedom from fear. When reevaluating my childhood, I realized I never felt safe with either parent. I was afraid of my mom, the ticking time bomb that could explode at any time. Something so simple as telling her I was hungry or had a stomachache led to her frustration and I felt it. It felt impossible to express how I felt, what I was feeling, or what I needed. When I tried, it wasn't perceived well. She always had a hardcore demeanor about herself while hiding her vulnerability. Sad to say, the older I got the more I understood why she was the way she was as I transformed and became her.

My father on the other hand I had a deep emotional connection with, and I always felt emotionally safe with him just not always physically safe. There was never that fear of talking to him, telling him how I felt even when it came to his addiction. From my childhood into adulthood, I shared everything with my father and never felt judged, afraid, or like I was a burden. His only issue was the addiction and I understood it was like a sickness, but I never felt nothing but genuine love from him.

The majority of my life I never wanted to disappoint anyone. I feared rejection and was afraid to ask questions. I never wanted to appear difficult so I would just go with the flow. People pleasing at its worst. Horney explained how parents undermine their children's security and induce hostility. A few examples I found relevant to my experiences were unfair punishments, erratic behavior, unkept promises, ridicule, and humiliation. According to Horney, when the safety and security of children are undermined, the child feels the need to repress the hostility. The repression occurs due to reasons of helplessness, fear of the parents, need for genuine love, or guilt. There was definitely the fear of my mother and the need for genuine unconditional love from her.

Horney further explains that children can become fearful of their parents through the form of punishment, physical abuse, or subtle forms of intimidation. Although I received whoopings like most children did, I didn't consider it physical abuse. I'm not saying that it was right; however, in my opinion in seems quite common within the Black household. Intimidation, on the other hand, was more so my experience. When it comes to the "repressed hostility" according to Horney it is manifested into a condition called basic anxiety!!

Basic anxiety is a pervasive feeling of loneliness and helplessness, the foundation of neurosis (Schultz, 2016). In Horney's words we feel "small, insignificant, helpless, deserted, endangered, in a world that is out to abuse, cheat, attack, humiliate, and betray." As a defense against basic anxiety Horney describes four self-protective mechanisms: securing affection, being submissive, attaining power, and withdrawing. Horney further explains how the four self-protective mechanisms can become permanent parts of the personality known as the ten neurotic needs. As we began to use these self-protective mechanisms, which are essentially our way of coping with anxiety. We tend to overuse them to the point that they become embedded within us and we have convinced ourselves these needs must be met.

The neurotic needs consist of affection/approval, a dominant power, power, exploitation, prestige, admiration, achievement/ambition, self-sufficiency, perfection, and narrow limits of life. I personally identify with most of them; however, affection/approval has always been a huge struggle of mine. I spent most of my life seeking the approval of others, especially my mother, longing to be understood, acknowledged, and have my love reciprocated. I would fall into these constant loops of me always trying to prove my worthiness to others. It led me to people pleasing while neglecting my own wants and needs. I settled for a lot of unhealthy attachments, creating co-dependency and abonnement issues.

During my quest to find love, the relationships that I was choosing felt like they were chipping away at me mentally and emotionally each time. As a result, I became bitter, angry, and emotionally detached just like my mother. Suddenly the resemblance was deeper than just looks. Horney describes me as the detached personality, behaviors, and attitudes associated with neurotic trends of moving away from people, such as a tense need for privacy. I strived for self-sufficiency and perfection because people are unreliable and full of disappointments. This is what I considered my protection strategy, protection from abandonment, disappointments, as well as judgements of others. I struggle with asking for help or asking for anything for that matter, which stems from the need to have power, control, and perfection. I also fear rejection which leads to me not getting the help that I may need. I became withdrawn and enjoyed spending time alone. I needed my alone time to regroup to calm my spirit down because people drained my energy! Until then, I had no idea I was neurotic! The neurotic self-image does not coincide with reality, it's real and accurate to the person who created it. That would be me at times. I have an overactive mind! Often, I have an over critical outlook of myself and my environment. I struggle trusting others as well as myself at times. The things that make me anxious are things that shouldn't cause anxiety and there's no real threat, yet I perceive most things or situations as a heightened threat.

Anxiety disorders are similar to mood disorders due to the partial characteristics of difficulty regulating negative effects in response to an anticipated threat (Herres et al., 2021). I try to tell my mind to relax don't be anxious, but my body does the opposite. My body tenses up because I'm trying to control it, my heart starts racing, I start to sweat, my mouth gets really dry, and I start trembling from the inside until it makes its way to the surface. Then my hands start to shake, and my voice gets shaky and high pitched as well. My words may become boggled as I try to gather my thoughts, control my tone, and movements. In my mind, I'm wondering do the people around me notice. I tell myself stay calm and look normal, take slow deep breaths, pronounce your words, slow down as I start to count backward in my head. The neurotic has little self-confidence because of insecurities and anxiety. Horney suggest that the neurotic self-image is like a house filled with dynamite, and always ready for self-destruction. Not only did I realize this was me, but it was also my mother!

DEAR DIARY

I DON'T WANT *to go back to how I use to be. I don't want to stay the way I am either. I just want to be better and truer to God and myself, Amen.* This was a prayer I wrote down and repeated every night. At some point I became so fed up with life, failed relationships, and lack of self-love that I began writing again. Writing has always been my outlet for my unspoken thoughts and emotions. This time it wasn't poetry, it was just pages of written tears of overwhelming emotions, questions of how and why, prayers for healing, self-reflection, and depression. Every day or every other day I began journaling in hopes of releasing the pain that had become unbearable. I was so unhappy with the person I saw when I looked in the mirror as she became increasingly unrecognizable. My first entry was March 6, 2014. I had just ended a relationship with a guy I had known for years but had only been in relationship with for less than six months. The reason it hurt so bad was not because I loved him but because I trusted him, and he made a fool out of me.

I was introduced to him by my mother years ago because she thought he would be perfect for me. Yes, she was wrong. Years had gone by since we first met. There were occasional phone conversations every once in a while, checking up to see how I was doing or rather or not I was single. However, we were both always in a relationship. Fast forward to maybe three years later, word got out to him that I was single and no longer with my child's father. Yes, me and my child's father broke up after sixteen years! Anyway, he got in touch with me through one of my sisters, only to come along and disrupt my entire life. Yes, I know I sound dramatic or should I say neurotic. I was highly upset at how everything played out. The audacity of this man! He really did disrupt my life and my healing process!

At the time I wasn't dating or entertaining anyone's worthless son. I had been celibate for a little over a year. I was minding my own business, adapting to my new career as a respiratory therapist, and taking care of my child. For the first time in my life, I was truly focusing on me. I had just moved into my first apartment by myself with my daughter and my niece and I was killing this miss independent, single mom life. I had done so much healing (so I thought) and came so far since my last relationship. When he came along, I was like, "Okay I'm completely open to dating now." I let my guards down thinking this man found me after all these years and we're both single. Is God trying to tell me something? My daughter and niece absolutely adored him and my family did as well. He came in strong, although he worked six days a week, he still made time for me. I met his son, we went on dates, on my off days we talked on the phone all day while he was working. He would cook for me. We spent the night at each other's home just enjoying one another's company. We went shopping together; he made my life so exciting, and I was finally happy. We didn't have to be out all the time we just enjoyed spending quality time with one another. Finally, God had sent me a man that was worth my time, serious, and upfront about what he wanted, and it was a bonus that I already knew him. Wrong, wrong, wrong! This man had every trait of the devil.

Yes, I'm being dramatic again, but he came like a thief in the night, lied, stole my mind, my heart, my time, and my body and deceived me. It was all lies and I found out he was living a double life. The man even had another woman that he was dealing with that stayed around the corner from me. I literally saw him dropping her off one day at the corner. People that can live those double lives like that are relentless. I don't have the mental capacity, time, or energy to try to deceive one person let alone two or three. Yet this man managed to fool the hell out of me and my mother!

Now, my child's father who I was with for sixteen years broke my heart several times and was a serial cheater, but we started out so young. This right here was different. I was older in my early thirties, independent, minding my own business, and he came right along and disrupted my inner peace. Why was this happening to me? Of course, I broke up with him and sat all his stuff he had at my house outside in

Aldi bags including his turkey fryer that he loved so much! I was hurt and embarrassed! Embarrassed that I allowed this man to deceive me! It was not easy trying to shake it off. To hell with my heart, I had created a soul tie!!

March 6, 2014,

Lord, please release me from this soul tie!!!

My heart was broken, and my ego was bruised. How did I allow this to happen? I knew it was just too good to be true. I allowed this man to come into my life and make himself comfortable. I allowed myself to be completely open and vulnerable with this man. I had to pray my way through this pain. I started this journal with hopes of writing the vision and God bringing it to pass. I went to church, took notes, studied scriptures, read self-help books, did a lot of self -reflection. I worked a lot of overtime to distract myself from the pain. Now, I know this sound's familiar to someone and if not consider yourself blessed. I even threw away everything he gave me including some diamond cluster stud earrings. This was serious!! I researched how to get rid of a soul tie and it said throw away everything that was tied to that person including gifts and cards. So that's what I did. I threw everything away, deleted every picture out of my phone, blocked him of course, and tried to move on.

My daughter was so disappointed. She even sent him a long text message saying she missed him and how she had never seen her mom so happy, and she believed we belonged together. That was the hardest part for me, trying to pretend I was okay in front of my daughter and niece when I was angry and deeply hurt. I tried to hide my tears and pain from them, but they knew I wasn't ok. She was hurting because her mom was hurting and tried to fix it herself. This made me even more angry because it wasn't just my emotions he played with; it was also my daughter and niece's.

During this time, my mom had moved to Atlanta, and I wasn't sure how I felt about that. Not only was I dealing with a heart break, but I was missing my mother. Surprisingly, I missed her presence and craziness. Our relationship was better. We had gotten to a point where my sisters and I would just hang out at my mom's house on the weekends and enjoy each other. She actually looked forward to having her four girls together as well. Knowing that she was right around the corner from me gave me a sense of relief. I felt an unexplainable personal closeness and comfort to her. It was like having her close but not too close. Plus, this pain I was experiencing was actually her fault (joking). The days just seemed so long. I was barely eating or functioning. What I came to realize was that I was slowly falling into a deep depression and trying everything not to allow it to overtake me, distracting myself with work and praying my way out was the plan.

Will I find the one thing I really want? Does it exist, that happily ever after marital bliss? Have I missed Mr. Right or have I made to many mistakes that wasn't right? How did they find love, while I'm still searching, getting colder and colder I'm so heartbroken! While bits and pieces of me are chipping away, my own self-reflection in a mirror that I barely even recognize. Should I stay? Or should I just give up? Does he exist? Or did I miss? Will love ever find me? Is God preparing me for him and him for me? How will I know when we cross paths, or will I forever be in search trying to control my own destiny?

I wrote that passage May 29, 2014, at work reflecting on all the mistakes I made while single looking for love, reflecting on poor life's decisions. Asking myself why was I so eager for love? Why is it that everyone else had seemed to have found love except for me? If I'm such a great woman, why has God forsaken me? Even this man that has hurt me so bad and deceived me has found love. You mean to tell me he gets to go on about his life and be happy while I suffer in silence? Like really, God, come on now! You even blessed my mother with a husband. I wish I could say I had learned my lesson by then, but my journal became full of more disappointments, heartbreaks, wasted time, by my own stupidity, ignorance, and desperateness. Although there were none I allowed to cause me that level of pain again I was high-functioning with a broken wounded heart. The last thing I needed was a man in my life. I was too broken and vulnerable.

I gave myself enough time to heal after my daughter's father (so I thought), but the other guy just sent me on a whole new emotional roller coaster with infinite loops and my head was still spinning. I wasn't over it; I was still hurt and begin to add pain on top of pain, disappointment on top of disappointment. I started recklessly sharing my body with men I knew were not for me, but I had convinced myself that temporary companionship was better than none at all. Not only was I hurt, angry, bitter, and resentful; I was like a shell, empty inside!

As I started to deal with the pain instead of running and distracting myself, I realized during my reflection I had daddy issues. It occurred to me that my relationship with my father as a child, and what he showed me, was a product of my adult relationships. As a child, my dad loved me, but he constantly lied, deceived me, used me at times, and told me that things would be different. But they never were. I loved him so much and tried to change him. I defended him to others, made excuses for him, stood by him— in a way I tried to protect him. Yes, he was a drug addict. Yes, he was a thief. Yes, he was a liar, but there was potential there. He had a big heart and despite his addiction and all these things, I knew he loved me. I hoped that my love, loyalty, and faithfulness would eventually change the man that he was. Praying that he would choose me over the drugs. He would see how much pain his actions caused me and just stop. So much like my adult relationships hoping I would be enough to make them change. Trying to prove that I was worth the change! I've spent my whole life looking for and needing acceptance from others, especially men and even with my mother. "The hurt and lack of love will continue if you don't make time to heal." "You change for two reasons. Either you learn enough that you want to, or you've been hurt enough that you have to." Both quotes were from my pastor. He was definitely talking to me. I began to cry out Lord help me to move on mentally and emotionally. I'm tired of making the same mistakes. I don't want to rely on a man or anyone to feel good about myself and enjoy the life that you have given me. Help me to make better choices and hold out for who and what you have for me.

October 16, 2016, it's 6 a.m. and I'm in a familiar place that I seem to visit at least once a year for a season. A place of loneliness, brokenness, defeat, depression, shame, and guilt. No one knows what I actually go through and how affected I am by life's disappointments, the disappointments of others and my own bad decisions. As I smile through my pain, I come to realize I really don't have my life figured out the way I thought I did. I have no idea what I'm doing, and it shows. I'm literally living in survival mode. I walk around like I'm so well put together, and I have everything under control. I pretend like nothing bothers me, and I don't need anyone. I'm content as long as I'm working and providing, the bills are getting paid, and my child is taken care of. Well, the truth is I'm not okay, everything bothers me, I overthink every situation, my mind is constantly in fight or flight mode. The bills are getting paid, but I can't save a dime because I'm excessively shopping to deal with my pain and calling it "retail therapy."

I'm an emotional mess, on the verge of having a mental breakdown. I'm desperately seeking love while being reckless with my heart, I can barely function on a day-to-day basis,

I'm always nervous, anxious and I'm just lost, confused, hurt, and scared. I do need people in my life, but I've been so disappointed I have trust issues to the point I don't even trust myself. I don't trust myself to make rational decisions. I don't trust myself to date. At this point I don't trust myself to even know what is best for me anymore. If I did, I wouldn't be feeling the way I do and I wouldn't be dealing with half the crap that I have allowed to happen. I'm completely disgusted with my own poor judgment and mistakes. With all of this going on inside of me, I'm trying to do my best to hide it from my daughter so that I don't project my issues off on her. I need to provide a physically and emotionally healthy environment for her no matter what! If I don't do anything else right, I have to be a good mom. I have so much work to do within myself and I don't know where to start. Lord help me!!!

DEAR DIARY
PART 2

EVERYONE IS NOT disposable. All of these pages are full of heartbreak, mistakes, and disappointments. I pray God turns my life around. It has to be better days ahead. Why am I like this? No amount of makeup, nice clothes, and money can fix the pain that I'm feeling inside. I don't even know what's wrong with me or why I'm so miserable and unhappy. There are people out here with far worst problems then me so why am I overreacting? Why can't I get out of whatever it is that I'm in? This was clearly not all about a man. I believe this was my turning point when I realized it was way deeper than my failed relationships. It was something inside of me missing and broken and I had no idea how to fix it.

My sister Kia said something that really made sense and stuck with me. She said you're a beautiful, intelligent successful woman you should be more selective about the men you date and raise your standards. Here I was trying to be an equal employment dater. It kind of hurt my feelings to hear my little sister say this because it was obvious even, she noticed that I was a mess, and clearly had lost control. It's one thing for you to know that your life is in shambles and a mess but when others notice your shortcomings— the shame, embarrassment, and guilt hits differently. Especially when you have tried to basically fake it until you make it while convincing yourself that you have everything under control.

At some point, I had completely lowered my standards and convinced myself it was ok. I tried to see the potential in people. I allowed people access to me that was neither qualified nor deserving. I was conducting my dating-love life like it was baseball— three strikes and then I was done. When in reality, they shouldn't have even been in the game!! Hell, I shouldn't have even been in the game. Clearly, I didn't know what I was doing. My judgment was clouded. Yes, I would cut people off rather quickly, but the problem was I shouldn't have even entertained the idea to even start with. My self-worth felt like it was at an all-time low!!!

During this time, I had decided to go back to school to pursue nursing. I was unhappy at work and of course in my personal life. I needed a change; I wanted a change. I also needed a new distraction from my pain. I decided to take a few classes both online and on campus. I continued working full-time night shift while juggling being a mom and trying to appear normal. I had a lot going on, which was exactly what I wanted so I didn't mind. I had passed three out of the four required classes already. I took the entrance exam, passed, and was officially accepted to the accelerated BSN (Nursing) program at Olivet University. During that time, I was saving money and time. I was so busy there was no time to feel lonely or do any purposeless dating or shopping. I only had school, work, and parenting. The only thing left to do was apply for my loans a month before the program started and finish my pathophysiology class within two months of starting my nursing classes. No problem I can do it!

Unfortunately, nursing school didn't work out. After all my challenging work and actually getting accepted, I couldn't get a private loan to pay for school, which was $55,000. After financial aid and regular loans, I still needed $28,000. I applied everywhere and no one would approve me. Talk about devastation. I suffered for two semesters juggling school and work for nothing. Like, God, I thought we both agreed this was the next step? I prayed about it before I even started, and I thought you had given me the go ahead? You allowed me to take these classes and pass with good grades and continue to work full time for nothing? I thought to myself, *okay this has to be a test to see how bad I really want it!*

As I processed what was going on, I convinced myself it was just a test. I won't give up God is just teaching me a lesson on perseverance I just have to find another way. I think God is just trying to prevent me from going into debt. That has to be it no other explanation!

Sunday morning came along and I needed answers. Lord what am I supposed to do now? My pastor preached a great sermon and of course I took notes.

"When you're broken, you're looking for anything to stop the pain, a quick fix. That's why the new relationship looks like the last relationship. You didn't take time to address the problem (you). Pain is a sign that something is wrong. God uses brokenness/pain to get our attention. When we suffer mental, emotional, and physical pain that's God saying deal with this! God targets the area of your life that needs to be broken. He also targets the area that you think you're the strongest because you think you don't need him."

Could it be my pride, my rebellious spirit, my need for control? Which is why my soul is so restless. Obviously, my dating life/love life or lack of needed to be broken!! I wasn't dating with purpose. Yes, I told myself I was looking for Mr. Right, my future husband but what I wanted, what I was allowing and how I was presenting myself was not lining up. Neither were the men I dated. So, I was out here with a dream, no action plan, and just going with the flow— constantly asking, "Lord, is this the one?" Meanwhile, God was like first of all you need to sit down somewhere because you not ready. Secondly, why would I send you a man who is unsure about you, marriage, or himself. I am not the author of conflict nor confusion. Plus, I didn't send the last two, but you swear it was me. Do you really know me or my voice? Matthew 6:33, *"But seek first his kingdom and his righteousness, and all these things will be given to you as well."* Luke 11:9, *"Ask, and it will be given to you; seek and you will find; knock and the door will be opened."* I must've been knocking on the wrong doors and asking for the wrong thing. Clearly my prayers were falling on deaf ears.

UGLY TRUTHS

Boundaries according to psychology are limits people set in order to create a healthy sense of personal space. Boundaries can be physical or emotional in nature, and they help distinguish the desires, needs, and preferences of one person from another. According to an article in "Good Therapy" boundaries are influenced by our culture, upbringing, and life experiences. For so long I avoided setting healthy boundaries for fear of rejection. I had to learn it's okay to be the bad person sometimes in order to protect my peace. How can you expect a person to adhere to a set quality of standards if you haven't made it clear and established healthy boundaries. You show people how to treat you and what you're willing and not willing to tolerate. I expected people to know how to treat me and talk to me based off my emotions and how I treated others. I believed it was universal that you do unto others as you want others to do unto you. Well, I've learned it doesn't quite work like that. People are so different and have been raised differently. They have become accustomed to their own experiences and what they've seen within their family units. Unfortunately, we don't all possess the same morals or core values, which can lead to unspoken boundaries often getting misconstrued!

I no longer want to be bound by the opinions of others. I've spent my entire life trying to please others while seeking their approval and neglecting my own emotions, wants, and needs. I dismissed my own morals and values and got further away from Christ and the core of who I was as a woman. I allowed myself to settle too many times because of fear. Fear of rejection, fear of being alone, fear of abandonment. My only goal now is to please God and I want him to continue to love me and teach me to love myself even through my imperfections. I can't live my life like everyone else. God didn't make me like everyone else. I love differently, I grieve differently, I mourn people and things differently. I'm a very emotional person and my heart cannot handle what I've allowed my flesh to do, and I keep hurting myself. At some point, I felt lost completely. It was apparent that I was suffering with anxiety and depression, but I needed to do something about it and stop having this pity party. What should I do? No one understands nor realizes I'm breaking— not even my mother. I was tired of procrastinating with my mental health and well-being. I wasted so much time overthinking and playing back the shame and guilt I felt due to failed relationships, childhood trauma, and insecurities. I haven't honored God the way that I should've. My life doesn't reflect a woman of God who is patiently waiting and trusting whatever season he has me in. Why am I so impatient and impulsive. I want to be better! I want to be productive in all areas of my life. I want to take back ownership of my mind and my heart. I want to fully surrender my life to Christ! Going to church, taking notes, and reading my bible wasn't enough. I needed to trust God. I needed to apply His word. Live His word, read, and speak the word over my life. I needed help! Both in a spiritual aspect as well as mentally and physically.

I was at work one evening overnight and I had a verbal altercation over the phone with a pediatric nurse. I was working in the blood gas lab, and I was alone in the department and everyone else was out doing their rounds seeing their patients. The nurse insisted that she had sent a blood gas of a child that I never received. She called about the results, and I had no results to report because I never received the sample. She was extremely rude and accused me of lying and being incompetent. I remained professional with my words of course, or so I thought but when I get mad, I get defensive and my voice gets very high pitched; I sound angry, my tone changes, and I tend to get louder. After hanging up the phone, I was so upset and agitated that I was uncontrollably shaking. I began having a full panic attack that had been triggered by my anger from a situation that really wasn't that bad. I was breathing heavily as if I had just run a marathon. It was hard to catch my breath as my respiration increased and my heart started racing. Suddenly, as my body temperature started to rise, I began to feel extremely hot. Although I was alone in the department, I felt so embarrassed that I lost control. I'm always trying to appear calm and relaxed even when I'm not. However, all of that goes out the window whenever I'm in confrontation of any kind, which is why I try to avoid it. I stopped everything I was doing and sat down, trying to coach myself to breath normal and take slow deep breaths. This was usually how I would instruct my patients when they were having an exacerbation of any kind and couldn't breathe. Well guess what, it's not that easy!

Eventually I was able to compose myself. I began to assess the situation and I thought to myself if this could happen from a phone conversation, I was afraid of what could've happened if we were actually face to face. I probably would've lost my job or at least been written up. This is why I avoid confrontation because the anger just takes over me. This was the first time something like this had happened to me at work. The panic attack was also new and something I'd never experienced.

Once I was able to control my breathing and my hands were functionable again, I got on the internet to find help. I went to ZocDoc and searched for a psychiatrist in my area that could see me as soon as possible. At that moment, I realized my anxiety had gotten so bad it was affecting my job. Not only was my anxiety getting worse, but I had anger issues as well that I couldn't control. I didn't know if my anxiety was causing the anger, or the anger was causing the anxiety. I mean, I've dealt with difficult people and conflict before. My first job was in customer service at a retail store for years. I had people curse me out daily and threaten me as well. All this anger projected toward me because they didn't like the return policy. I had people tell me they would be waiting for me after closing time, and I didn't care at all. I had never been affected like this before and that was verbal abuse face to face. What was happening to me?

I found a psychiatrist in St. Charles, Illinois which was about fifty minutes away from me, but I didn't care. She specialized in anxiety disorders and was able to see me that same week. I filled out the required documentation, booked my appointment, and anxiously awaited confirmation, all while working during the middle of the night. That next day, I kept checking my email for confirmation. I'll never forget my first appointment with her. She made me cry and I never even opened up to her. The anticipation of going to see her was overwhelming! I kept replaying the day in my head over and over. I was still battling with the disappointment from my lack of control at work. I kept thinking about what I could've done differently that possibly could've produced a different outcome. An outcome that didn't leave me racing to a psychiatrist office to get help. Regardless of how I had gotten there, I needed to be there. I just knew I was about to get fixed!!

In my mind, I was just there to get medication to help with anxiety and mood swings that's it. Diagnose me, write me a prescription, and send me on my way! I didn't think I needed therapy at the time. I just wanted a quick fix. When

I arrived, of course I had to wait for her because doctors are never ready at your scheduled appointment time. As I was waiting, a teenage male and what I assumed was his mother came out of her office as she walked them to the front. As we made eye contact, she called my name, and proceeded to take me to the back. I thought to myself, o*k do she see adults because I'm only a child of God. I got real issues going on here. Maybe this was a mistake.*

I walked into her office, looked around, and noticed there was no couch. She had me to sit in a chair in front of her desk. I expected to get comfortable on her couch like they do in the movies with my feet up and arms crossed! Hmm, I guess this chair would do. I remember she asked me, "What brings you in today?" I told her all about my panic attack at work and my anxiety. As she began to take notes on her notepad, she asked how long I had been feeling this way and when did I first notice it was a problem. I replied expressing how I think I've always had the anxiety well before I knew what it was; however, I had never experienced a panic attack before. She then said, "Why don't you tell me about your childhood?" First, thing that came to my mind was she a child psychiatrist? What does my childhood have to do with right now and this prescription I need? All I heard was my mother's voice in my head saying, "Don't tell that lady my business. What happens in my house stays in my house!" So, I smiled and said my childhood was great and normal. I refused to go into details. I didn't feel the need to tell her anything about my childhood. I mean it's not like you can change the past anyway. So, I just smiled and gave vague answers, lied a little or embellished and then suddenly, I just started crying uncontrollably.

She knew exactly what she was doing. She saw right through me. I believe in my heart and soul I just wanted to cry out and tell the truth, but I couldn't. I wasn't there for that; I just needed a prescription to make me all better. I thought to myself, *if I wanted to discuss my problems, I would go to a therapist but instead I came to you because you are a doctor, and you can prescribe medication and a therapist cannot. So, please fix me!!* I did open up about mental illness running on my father's side of the family and maybe it was possible that I may be experiencing my own mental health crisis. She explained to me how it's a chemical imbalance and sometimes people need therapy and/or medication and that it was okay. A chemical imbalance doesn't fix itself, but medication can help. She wrote me a prescription and scheduled me for another appointment in three weeks. I left her office feeling some relief and empowered. I was so excited. I was finally getting the help I thought I needed. I just knew I was about to be cured of all my issues!

"Living with anxiety is like being followed by a voice. It knows all your insecurities and uses them against you. It gets to the point when it's the loudest voice in the room. The only voice you can hear," (Gluck, 2013)

As time went on, I saw her a couple more times. I never gave her too much information, just enough to appear compliant so that she would continue to give me refills. She would only give me a prescription for thirty days. I was taking my medication just like I was supposed to, and I felt different. I was in a good mood; I didn't feel so overwhelmed with life. I felt more energetic. I wasn't waiting for the day to be over. By no means was life perfect but it didn't seem so bad. Life was more manageable on the medication. I wasn't so angry or easily irritated. I felt normal. I felt in control again.

I remember talking to my friend about how I was feeling much better and had more control over my emotions. Her reply was, "You don't need any medication. You just need to pray more and ask God to deliver you." Listen, that sounds great and all but that's the last thing someone with anxiety, depression, or any mental illness who is fighting to keep it all together wants to hear. What made her think I hadn't done that already? Apparently, prayer was not enough. That's just like someone having diabetes or high blood pressure. Would you just keep encouraging them to pray about it instead of going to the doctor and seeking help? Yes, prayer works but I needed a prescription! By no means was that all I needed but it was an essential start!

Seeing a psychiatrist was expensive and I wasn't even reaping the full benefits. I eventually stopped going and that was mainly because my primary doctor said she would continue the prescription for me. I actually talked more to her about my life and problems than I did the psychiatrist. One day at my annual appointment, I told her all about my psychiatrist. She continued to say good for you taking control of your mental health. She then offered to take over my prescription as long as I felt comfortable on the medication and felt like it was working, which I did so that's what we did. No more taking that fifty-minute drive to sit in her uncomfortable chair and avoid confronting my real issues and then receiving a bill for it.

Now, here's the problem that a lot of people may run into, especially when dealing with their mental health. The medication works so well that we stop taking it, assuming we've been cured or convincing ourselves we don't need it. It's like, ok I feel great now. I think I can handle it from here! No more pills! Now, that may be the case for some and usually that's considering you've done the work. You've made progress in therapy, and you've confronted your issues and progressed forward with things under control.

Clearly that was not my experience. I hadn't done any real work nor confronted anything! I was merely looking for a quick fix and just wanted a miracle pill. I had a good run for about eight to ten months off the medication and then I was right back where I started. My anxiety was out of control and depression right there front and center. By the way, you should never just stop taking your medication without consulting with your doctor and being properly weaned off. If you go to the doctor and I hope you all do, you ever notice they always ask you about your mental health? Have you had any depression or thoughts of suicide? Well yes and no, I was right back at my doctor's office like, *yea I think I need to restart my prescription again!* Of course, she wrote me a new prescription. I think I gave it a fair chance but somehow I was not getting the same effect as I did the first time. It felt like my mental high was over!!

With things not going the way I had hoped for, my doctor recommended a different medication. She prescribed Zoloft, which is also an antidepressant medication. Before I was taking Paxil. She also added another medication Propranolol, which happens to be a beta blocker usually used for blood pressure. However, it also treats anxiety symptoms such as tremors, sweating, and dry mouth. Somewhere during my journey, I developed essential tremors as my doctor called them. Yes, the shaky hands were here to stay and had gotten worse. Although the medication helps tremendously, it's definitely not a cure. Life is just more manageable with it. My tremors didn't stop completely but they weren't as noticeable, and I was able to physically manage better. Plus, I was able to start back getting my nails done! I still would have days I questioned my mental health asking why I can't just be normal like most people. Who the heck needs a pill just to have a spa day? However, over the years I have discovered most people are not what society has deemed as "normal." Especially in health care. The level of stress that we encounter on a daily basis is bound to take a toll on you. If it doesn't, consider yourself lucky. As for me, I may have already been genetically predisposed. You would be surprised how many people suffer with their mental health and ignore the signs within and try to self-medicate with drugs, alcohol, and even sex!

You have people that make excuses for their behavior and justify it by saying, "This is just who I am," or "I've always been like this." When in reality there very well could be some mental illness and instability. You may wonder why your thought process doesn't always make sense., You seem impulsive, always angry, moody, irritated, and paranoid, it could be a chemical imbalance. By no means I am a doctor but all I'm saying is it doesn't hurt to talk to someone. I'm not saying get on ZocDoc like I did and find you a psychiatrist but start by talking to your primary doctor. Do a self-evaluation and be honest with yourself. You may just have a chemical imbalance and need medication and or therapy!

NEW BEGINNINGS

JUNE 30, 2017, I closed on my very first home by myself.
I was excited, scared, overjoyed, and of course anxious. That
was such a long tedious process! I looked at so many houses
and put in so many offers and lost out on every last one! As
time went on, my area of interest went further and further
away from the west suburbs. My sudden urge to purchase
a home was the result of being disappointed that I could
not get a private loan for $28,000 to go back to school,
yet I was approved for a $190,000 house loan. Becoming
a homeowner was definitely part of my future goals but I
wanted to go back to school first. I guess God had other
plans for me instead. Anyway, during this time I was single, celibate again, focused, medicated, and on my healing
journey again. I felt great!!

I paid off some bills, got my credit score up, saved up a
good amount of money, and purchased me and my baby our
very first single-family home. I was so proud of myself! Yes,
I would have liked to purchase a home with my husband

and not have to worry about the upkeep of a home by myself but hey, at the rate I was going I might retire before that happens. My daughter was no longer a baby she was actually sixteen at the time. Although I was late in securing us a home of our own, she was still able to benefit somewhat from growing up in a family home. Even if the family was just her and I. I wanted her to have some memories of a childhood home, a backyard to relax in, family get togethers, having our own BBQs, and occasionally entertaining. I even purchased her a dog since we couldn't have one in our apartment. A house is not a home without a puppy. Not having to go to the laundromat was priceless, not having to deal with tenants over your head, or just people period was priceless. Never having to get a parking spot or parallel park was an added bonus. The stability and level of accomplishment that I felt was amazing. It also did great things for my mental health as well.

Of course, I wasted no time furnishing my new home but first I did minor cosmetic renovations. I also bought all new appliances stainless steel of course and had the entire upstairs painted and then it was time to furnish. Even my mother had to admit I had done well, and she was so proud of me. I can only remember three occasions when I felt like I had made her proud. The day I graduated high school, the day I graduated from college in my Respiratory Program, and now the purchase of my first home.

I had the housewarming in August after I got everything together and presentable. My mom was actually visiting from Atlanta during that time, so it was perfect. I was so excited to have her there with me. Anyone that knows my mother knows she has a good eye for décor, and it didn't stop there. She was a landscaper as well! She could make anything look good and on a budget! Shortly after my housewarming, which was a success, my mom informed me that she needed to stay with me for a short while. This was when I discovered her cancer had returned, and she wanted to be treated by her original doctor that diagnosed her here in Oak Park.

Of course, that was not a problem and obviously I was concerned about her. I was happy to share this new beginning with my mother by my side. It was the perfect opportunity to get her help, especially for my backyard that was absolutely horrible. Plus, I get to keep an eye on her at the same time. Now, I had just seen my mother in April when my sisters and I along with our children went to visit her for her birthday. It had only been four months since I had seen her last. During that time, she was at her normal weight and her normal crazy self. There was no indication that something was wrong, nothing at all seemed different about her. She looked the way she's always looked and appeared like her normal self. Now here we are only four months later and not only had she told us her cancer was back, but there was also a huge drastic visual change in her appearance.

She had lost a ton of weight she had to be about 110 pounds at this time, which I've never seen her that small before! Her skin was darker than normal. I was concerned but I didn't want to appear overly concerned because I didn't know how she felt mentally and emotionally. So, I tried to act normal and not make a big deal of the situation. I remember talking to my sister, Kia, about it and saying that I felt like our mother wasn't going to be here with us in the flesh for too long. I hated to say that out loud, but God had showed it to me. I didn't want to speak death over my mother; I only wanted to speak life. That same week she had arrived; I had a dream I was at her funeral. I know she had beat cancer once ten years ago, and I was praying she could do it again. Aside from what I had seen in my dream and the drastic physical change, I was still hopeful and praying that this was just me overthinking and maybe it's not as bad as it looked. God does perform miracles. She beat cancer before, and she'll beat it again!!

As days turned into weeks and weeks turned into months, she appeared to be the same. She was still a strong and feisty woman. She would spend her time talking crazy to me, rearranging my house, breaking my one rule— which was no smoking in my house— and shopping. I hated cigarette smoke. It made it feel like I was struggling to breathe, especially if it's right in front of me. Plus, I didn't want that smell in my walls and furniture. While I was at home, she would go outside to smoke or in the garage. Once I would leave for work, she would do as she pleased. I remember my daughter telling me, "I told Grandma you said no smoking in here, but she said you don't tell her what to do," and she was right.

When I got off work in the mornings, I would cook us both a little breakfast. I would take her breakfast in the basement where she was staying because she refused to stay in the extra bedroom. She would come and go as she pleased and we would go shopping on my off days. As time passed, her appetite started to decrease more and she wasn't eating as much. She just wanted one egg and two pieces of bacon, and some days she couldn't even eat that.

My stepdad came in from Atlanta every week to take her to chemo. I loved seeing him come every week. He would take care of her, and I could get a mental break from her. I knew my mom was missing her husband and home, so it was good to see her content in those moments even when she tried to hide it. Overall, I honestly enjoyed looking after her. It felt good to take care of my mother. After all, I went to work every day and took care of other people's family members so of course I didn't mind taking care of my own mother.

Now, somewhere down the line in what felt like a short amount of time, things took a turn for the worst with our relationship and her health. Aside from her not respecting my boundaries, she began antagonizing me. Suddenly, the peace I had been working so hard to achieve was gone. She even started to create problems between my daughter and I, which was the last straw. She would say things like, "I see why you don't have a man," and telling my daughter I was miserable and depressed, discussing me in a negative way with her. I couldn't understand why she would discuss me like that with my child.

All of a sudden, all my emotions from my childhood started to resurface and I didn't know what to do. I felt like a helpless child again! The difference this time, I was an adult and this was my home and my child. I refused to allow her to treat me that way in my own home and manipulate me when I spoke out about it. I did the only thing I knew how to do I shut down, withdrew, and turned my emotions off the best way I could. I remember calling my dad and venting to him about everything like I did when I was younger. Of course, his answer was, "Put her ass out!!!" Well, that was not an option. She was still my mother, and she needed me right now. What I couldn't understand was considering everything that was going on with her health why was she acting this way toward me. I now know that when people are hurting and going through something they tend to lash out at the people close to them. She even created drama between my sisters. It wasn't fair to me or them but again this was my mother we're talking about!!!

In order for me to hold on to my sanity, avoid disrespecting her, and not turn my back on her when she needed me the most, I finally went to see a therapist. I was at work one evening and broke down to a childhood friend that I trusted and admired. After pouring my heart out to her she replied, "Have you ever tried counseling before?" I said, "Well yes and no." She then suggested Christian counseling. I'll never forget my first session she asked me what brought me in. I replied, "Well my mother lives with me, and she is driving me crazy, but she also has cancer and I'm not sure how long she will be with us. I can't talk to her, and I need a healthy outlet for my emotions. I also want to be able to forgive her for past pain as well as the current pain so that I can care for her with a clean heart and let go of my resentment." The therapist replied, "Everything reverts back to your childhood. Let's start there."

This time I didn't hold back. I needed help and I was ready to do the work and confront whatever issues that needed to be confronted. I felt like I was on borrowed time! I went to therapy for a little over two months with weekly sessions, which was expensive and I was paying out of pocket. Everything was focused on my mother, my childhood, and how do I forgive and move on in the midst of the current situation. I remember telling my therapist I knew my mom wasn't going to change so I needed to accept her for who she was as well as continue to care for her while controlling my own emotions. I would never disrespect her, but I was still holding on to so much anger and resentment from my childhood. All this time I thought I had healed from my childhood trauma and her moving in with me just brought it all back. I was like a child all over again trying to do my best to at least meet my mother's expectations while seeking her approval/validation and denying my own emotions. But I also had my own child I had to protect. I didn't want to be selfish considering all she was going through.

She criticized my parenting skills, my dating life, and how I chose to decorate my house. Why didn't I have a man and not married yet? What's wrong with your social life, what's wrong with your mental health? Why you always anxious I see you depressed too. I just felt like she was trying to mentally break me. My anxiety was manifesting through anger, isolation, and of course resentment. It was a lot to deal with. I was caught between trying to be supportive of her while ignoring what felt like attacks on me. I found myself overwhelmed. Being a mother myself, going to work and caring for others while barely holding on mentally myself. The attacks were nothing new but before when she started talking crazy I could just get up and say, "Alright mother I'm leaving" or say, "Ok I'll talk to you later," and hang up the phone. There was no escape this time, this was my home.

Unfortunately, just like a child/teen, I just had to deal with it and accept my peace was being compromised. It got so bad; I would just come home and stay in my room all day I would avoid her as much as possible just like I did as a child. One day, as I lay on my bed, watching the morning news, they did a segment about this organization and how they support the young moms. So, I Googled it and found more information including locations. I filled out an application to volunteer. I received an appointment, had a tour of the facility, attended a personal interview, and completed a background check.

During my free time, I began volunteering at the organization, which was called New Moms. They provided housing, childcare, parenting classes, and job training for teenage moms that became homeless. After everything was clear, I started volunteering on Tuesdays and Thursdays at

5 p.m. at the daycare center while the moms attended parenting classes and group therapy. I started volunteering as an escape from home and my own problems. I've always gotten pleasure out of helping and caring for others, plus it took my mind off my mother driving me crazy. I have discovered when you are struggling with depression or anything, try being a blessing to others. It's actually quite therapeutic. It didn't take long before I felt overwhelmed by the children at the main location, so I then switched it up between two different locations.

There was a brief moment when my mother had gotten cleared to return home to Georgia. I was so excited!! At first, she seemed like she didn't want to go home, and I didn't understand why. I remember getting off of work one morning and coming home to find her still there even though she had a flight to catch back home that morning. As she was laying down in the basement on the couch, I sat down in front of her and asked her why was she avoiding going home? She just ignored me. Then I said something that I wish I would have never said. I asked her was she afraid that she was going to die in Atlanta? And then she pulled her gun out from under her pillow and said, "Get out of my face." I said, "Really, Mom, you're going to pull your gun out?" She said nothing just looked at me with the gun pointed at me. I walked away confused about what had just happened and I realized that was exactly why she was avoiding going home.

She used to say all the time don't let me die in Georgia with them people. It made me wonder could this have been part of the reason she came to live with me. She eventually did go home to Georgia for a while and she called me and said some terrible things to me, and I just broke down and told her exactly how I felt. "I'm not a little girl anymore you can't manipulate me. My feelings do matter, and this is why I went to therapy." Why did I say that!! She was so upset with me. All this time I never told her I was in therapy and now I knew why. She didn't agree or approve of it. She told me, "If I knew you had to go to therapy just to deal with me, I would have never came to your house. You could have saved your time and money, and I could have left!!" And that's why I didn't tell her. Although we had never talked about therapy before, I knew she wouldn't have approved of me talking to a complete stranger about my problems, let alone telling her business. Even though that didn't go so well I was honest with my feelings, I didn't disrespect her, and I remained calm. How she perceived it was a different story. Going to therapy was ultimately about me and my mental health and wellbeing. I refused to allow her to make me feel bad for doing so.

Eventually, she ended up having to come back to stay with me. It was probably a few weeks later and things were different this time. She actually moved into the extra bedroom that I had prepared for her instead of taking over my basement area. I allowed her to smoke in the house, but I refused to buy her cigarettes. I was still seeing my therapist. One of my homework assignments from therapy was to write her a letter even if I didn't plan on giving it to her. So, I did and of course I didn't give it to her. I wrote a letter saying everything I wanted to say to her as a child but didn't have the guts to say or afraid of how she would respond.

Well, one day she came into my bedroom while I was reading and said she needed to talk to me. She sat at the edge of my bed and was very transparent and vulnerable, which I had never seen in her before that day. She told me about her childhood with her mother and how traumatizing it was, and she explained to me how she never really felt loved or respected by my grandmother. She talked about how she was the only girl growing up with three brothers and was forced to handle everything within the house as well as tend to the bills while my grandmother worked. She felt as if she favored her sons more and really didn't like her. She further shared how it made her feel like she was forced to be grown and handle adult responsibilities even though she wasn't the oldest and she had no choice but to adapt to become strong and tough. She talked about not really having a relationship with her father and how her mother's burdens became her burdens. She shared a memory with me that was obviously still causing her pain. She said she was out with her friends at a party not sure how old she was but how my grandmother came to the party looking for her. The hurtful part was she addressed her with what sounds like quite frequently as a bitch. Tears rolled down her face while we both sat there in silence.

I grabbed my pillow when I should have grabbed her. She sincerely apologized to me. She said, "Shanta, you were my first born and I didn't know what I was doing with you. I made a lot of mistakes, but I did the best I could and knew how to do. I didn't have the best example. If I owe anyone an apology it's you." I sat there paralyzed, hugging my pillow and afraid to move. My heart raced and I was breathing heavy with tears running down my face. We both were crying. I wanted so badly to reach out and grab her and hug her, but I couldn't. I just thanked her. I needed that. I then asked her what about my sister Kia? She quickly snapped and said, "I don't owe her anything her issues is with her father not me!" I said, "OK calm down I thank you for mines!"

My next session I discussed it with my therapist, and she asked me why I didn't hug her. My response was I just didn't feel safe enough to do so. Throughout my entire childhood into my adulthood, I had been told I was too sensitive, which I was but it wasn't necessarily a bad thing. But because I was made to believe it wasn't a good thing, overtime, I eventually conditioned myself to become numb to pain, criticism, and my emotions. Being vulnerable felt like being weak and I had to be strong. I could be crying inside and having a complete melt down, but I had learned not to show it. So, in that moment I was unable to return the gift of being vulnerable with my own mother. I felt like she had made me that way and sounds like her mother made her that way. I used the word gift because that's what it was. She gave me exactly what I needed all along in that moment.

I still feel to this day like I failed to return it. Why didn't

I reciprocate the vulnerability? I just said thank you and I love you too. Looking back on it, I regret not embracing that moment to connect with her. It was obvious I had become a wounded version of her. It's like we were on our third generation of damaged women. I am my mother, but it has to stop with me!!!

As time went on, my mother's health started declining to the point that she was struggling to walk and needed a cane, and she was starting to get confused. During that year, 2018, my sisters and I decided to throw a Mother's Day Bash to honor her. I felt like that could've been her last Mother's Day. We went all out for her. We invited all her friends, including people that had no idea what she was going through because she was such a private person. Her baby girl, Paris, came from Atlanta and my stepdad got the grill going. We had so much food; it was truly a feast.

The day of the party she walked around greeting everyone. When her energy got low, which didn't take long, she laid down on my futon in the family room and her friends just surrounded her, cried, and loved on her. Many of them were in complete shock because they were used to seeing this bold, strong, life of the party, huge personality. She no longer had the strength to be that person. Nevertheless, she was happy as could be considering the circumstances, which of course she didn't show it, but she enjoyed it.

I started taking on more responsibilities to care for her. After Mother's Day, her health declined even more. We were at the stage that she needed twenty-four-hour care and couldn't be left alone. Everyone stepped in and stepped up! My stepdad continued to come every week even though she had stopped going to chemo. My seventeen-year-old daughter stayed with her while I was at work overnight. We had a few of her friends that had just found out come and stay with her during the day and overnight as well. We had support from everyone, including old church members that had become family. I started giving her bed baths, oiling her down, toileting her, preparing her bed on a daily basis to keep her comfortable. I started buying things to accommodate the change. I purchased her sippy cups for her to drink out of because it was hard for her to hold a regular cup and lift it up to her mouth to drink. A bed rest pillow to help her sit up in bed and support her back. I would literally pick her up, carry her to the futon in the family room and lay her down while I changed her bedding weekly.

I remember her crying to me one day saying she was tired and ready to go. Then she told me, "Tell my husband to let me go" as we both cried. It was apparent that she was still fighting and holding on for my stepdad and my baby sister. She then said, "Take care of my husband Shanta and my baby Paris. They need me the most."

During my last therapy session, I told the therapist okay this is it; my mother needs me more than ever now. I have provided consistent continuous care and I have accomplished what I came to accomplish. I can fully focus on her now and set my own emotions aside to do whatever it is God needs me to do. I also informed her I would come back after God called my mother home because I knew I'd need her again for that pain. My therapist hugged me and told me she would be there. I was always going to care for her with or without the therapy, but I needed to do some work myself to prepare myself mentally and emotionally. I wanted to forgive my mother and have a clean heart. I wanted to be able to give of myself freely and I wanted her to feel my love and compassion for her.

My mother had stopped going to chemo because she had no strength left. She had pretty much stopped eating completely and occasionally would drink Ensure. I believe she was somewhere between eighty-five and ninety pounds. I also think that was her way of saying she had enough.

My skills as a respiratory therapist were tested on July 2018. I had just renewed my Basic Life Support (BLS) certification a couple days ago, and everything was fresh on my mind. My stepdad and sister were at a funeral, and it was just my mom, daughter, and myself at home. I had to work that evening, so I was asleep. My daughter ran into my room frantically and yelled, "Grandma throwing up blood and it's a lot." I immediately jumped up went into her room to check on her and it was a bucket of blood. I knew what was going on, so I called her oncologist and told her what was happening and asked her what she wanted me to do. She told me to bring her into the emergency department and she would meet us there. After I got off the phone with her, I told my mother what she said and her response was,

"Ok but I don't want to ride in an ambulance." I said, "No problem I will take you."

I got dressed and got her dressed then I picked her up because she couldn't walk, and I put her over my shoulder. That was how small she was. When I got to my car in the driveway, I opened the backseat door and I lowered her down to put her in the car and when I sat her down I noticed she had stopped breathing and her eyes were closed. I started shaking her and calling her name and there was no response. I did a sternal rub and still no response. I checked for a pulse and didn't feel one, but I wasn't confident because I was somewhat panicking inside as well and scared. I remember my trainer saying in class when in doubt just do the chest compressions so that's what I did. I took her out of the car and laid her down in the grass and started CPR. As I was doing CPR, I was yelling for my daughter to call 9-1-1. She came out hysterically crying and frantically calling but they couldn't understand her. Thank God my neighbor was home; she came out and took the phone and told them the address and what was going on. While still doing chest compressions on her small, frail lifeless body, I told myself today will not be the day, Lord!!! With blood around her mouth, I proceeded to give her mouth to mouth because if she survived this, I didn't want her to have a brain injury from lack of oxygen. So yes, from my lungs to hers I gave her mouth to mouth!!! As I continued with the CPR doing thirty compressions and then giving two breaths, my neighbor who knew my mom from childhood just yelled encouraging words. "Hold on Faye, fight Faye fight!! Don't leave us!!!"

The police arrived before the ambulance did and the officer took over chest compressions. As physically tired as I was, I would've passed out on top of her before I would've ever stopped!! The ambulance finally arrived, and one person took over for the police officer while the other questioned me. I took him into the house to her room, he looked at her medications, and we thought she may have taken an extra dose of morphine. I briefly gave him a medical history and what was happening prior to her cardiac arrest.

When we came back outside, they had put her in the back of the ambulance. I got into my car to follow them, but they didn't leave right away they were still sitting there while blocking my driveway. I thought to myself, *are they not moving because she's still coding and too unstable to leave?* At that moment, all I knew to do was to pray. They eventually pulled off after telling me which hospital they were going to. My mind was racing my tremors were suddenly out of control and I was scared! I called my stepdad and informed him, and he eventually met us at the hospital with one of my sisters.

When we all arrived at the hospital, we weren't allowed to go back and see her. They kept us waiting for a while and my stepdad decided it was time we discussed her code status. I remember what my mom had told me, but I wasn't sure if I should relay that to him. Emotions were high and we were all scared. They eventually allowed us to see her once she was stable. Believe it or not, that lady was a true fighter. She was awake, alert, and more importantly still with us!!! She didn't have to go on any life support machine. She was breathing on her own and spent one day in ICU and was back fussing the next day.

I saw an old coworker that was working in the ICU that evening. I introduced him to my mom and asked him to keep an eye on her. That next day, he messaged me on Facebook and said, "Your mother is definitely a character and full of life!" When we all went to visit her the following day, she kept saying, "Get me out of here and take me to where my doctor is." It was like music to my ears! She was complaining, noncompliant, and stressing the whole hospital staff out and I loved it! Every person that walked into her room she wanted me to tell them how I saved her life. Her words were, "Tell them how you was doing them chest compressions and fractured my ribs and now my chest hurt." Then she had the nerve to say, "Yea I think she was thinking about her childhood and tried to break my ribs." In case you hadn't figure it out, she had a great sense of humor as well, it was a little dark sometimes, but she was funny.

I was so happy God decided to give us more time with her. When she was released, we all just loved on her and appreciated having her in the land of the living. It's funny how during that time of me resuscitating my mother I felt no anxiety, I had no tremors while doing it. I was able to think clearly and do what needed to be done. Kind of like when I'm at work. She was grateful for me, and I was grateful for her. There was nothing I wouldn't have done for her regardless of how much she got on my nerves. At the end of the day that was my mother, and I was her first-born child.

The bible speaks about honoring thy mother and father and that's what I've always tried to do. I may not have always been obedient or perfect, but I always respected her as my mother!! No matter how mad she made me at times, I would and could never curse her. Not only did she not raise me like that, nor would she have tolerated that. Plus, she would not be the reason my days on earth would be cut short! Exodus 20:12, "Honor your father and mother, so that you may live long in the land the Lord your God is giving you."

After that scare, my mother's health continued to decline and her doctor convinced her to go on hospice services. That was extremely hard for her to do and also for us to witness. We decided it would be best if she entered into hospice services at my home. She had a nurse that would come out a few times a week. She declined the help from the nurse's assistant, which was fine because I was her nurse assistant anyway.

As our new reality started to set in, my mother began telling my stepdad and myself her last wishes. She told us she wanted to be buried in a night gown because it was her final rest. She told us not to put a wig on her just a nice head wrap. She also said don't put all my business in that obituary. Folks are just too nosy so keep it simple. Lastly, she said don't give my car to no one just keep it. This lady still had jokes, but she was serious about that. My daughter later expressed to me that she was afraid that my mother would pass away in our home and if she did, she didn't think she could continue to live there. I took that into consideration and as weeks passed, she became more disoriented, so I called the hospice nurse to come out. My mother had started calling out to family members that had passed away. She also kept calling out a name that no one recognized. The nurse came to the house did an assessment and said she's getting close. At that time, we decided to admit her to the hospice ward in the hospital. When we got there, we discovered that the name that we didn't recognize was posted on the walls of the hospice unit. The person had actually been memorialized and the hospice ward was established in his name. Every day we went to visit. I would go before I went to work and just sit with her. My friends would visit and her friends came to visit. Each day was getting harder and harder. She stayed with us for almost a week.

August 15, 2018, God called my mother home, and she waited for me to get there along with my sisters to take her last breath. That morning, I had just gotten off work and my stepdad called and said, "Get here now. I don't think she has long." No matter how much I tried to prepare myself for that day, you can never really prepare yourself for the death of a loved one. Especially not your mother. God showed me the day was near when she first walked into my home, which was August of 2017. I knew it was going to happen but a part of me was still in some sort of denial. I was secretly still praying for a miracle. I had to; the strongest woman I knew that would stand up to any and everybody was being robbed of her life. If the crowd was going right, she was going left! She was a force to be reckoned with! She didn't need an entourage; she stood alone and proudly! She lived her life unapologetically!

She was more than my mother. She was a woman that had her own childhood traumas to deal with. A woman that had many obstacles and struggles as well but always made a way. She played the hand that God had given her that life had given her, and she never complained. She dried her own tears in private and stood firm on her faith. My mother was only fifty-six years old when she left us. She had so much more living and healing to do. Her first grandchild was going to prom and graduating high school soon. We never got to take that family portrait I had planned and talked about. We never got to take that family vacation together with all the grandkids. The last visit we had in Atlanta to see her she said, "I love you all, but I wish yawl had some men in your lives, it's boring with just you all coming alone to visit." She never got a chance to terrorize the men we have in our lives now. She may have been feisty, but she had a huge and strong but delicate heart. She wanted us to find love. The love that she had found with my stepdad. He stood by her until she took her last breath and did it so gracefully. As she would say she always looked out for the underdog and "to know me is to love me." She also would say, "I ain't never ran from a good fight." And she fought until the end!!

Although she was not perfect, she had done a lot of good

in her short lifetime. Regardless of whether you loved her or not you respected her! Believe it or not, in all her glory, she was a woman of God. She loved the word of God and would debate anyone about it. Even during her final days, she said out of her own mouth, "I could ask God why me, but why not me. Even Jesus suffered here on earth. Who am I to think I'm any different!" She was stubborn, proud, fearless— a true warrior. She was a lot of things to a lot of people, but she was my mother!

After losing my mom, even my father had a hard time dealing with it. When I notified him of her passing, he expressed how unfair life was. He felt as though he spent so much time in the streets and on drugs that he should've been the one to go first, plus he was ten years older than she was. As I tried to comfort him and persuade him not to think like that, he apologized for the way things were during his drug addiction. Crazy part is, I had forgiven him years ago. I understood that the addiction made him do things outside of his character and even then, I never doubted his love for me. My parents had lives way before I came into this world and ultimately, I honestly believe they did the best they knew how while fighting their own demons.

During this time, his health started to decline as well. The doctors found a tumor on his brain the same month my mom passed away. It wasn't cancerous but the doctors advised him to have it removed. Unfortunately, in the process they discovered his heart was weak and suddenly that took priority over the tumor of course. He ended up having a couple of heart attacks and began to deteriorate quickly. Constantly in and out of the hospital. With him in Alabama and me in Chicago, it was rough. I was able to visit a few times and it just made his day seeing my face. Eventually, his health had gotten so bad, and he needed around the clock care, so my grandmother put him in a nursing home. At first, he hated it, and it was hard for me to accept as well but it was the best option for him at the time. He eventually got used to it and called me and would tell me how he was drinking all the Ensure he wanted and assured me he was ok.

REFLECTION

I REMEMBER GOING to church one Sunday and the pastor said, "If everyone threw their problems in a big ole pile some of y'all might just grab yours back." My entire life I've convinced myself whatever it is I'm dealing with will be okay because it's always someone out there that has it worse than me. Although that is true, it doesn't mean my problems are any less significant. I also conditioned myself to expect the worst and hope for the best. It's hard to be disappointed if you expect the disappointment. I know it was a coping mechanism, which it did help me to cope but it probably wasn't the healthiest form of coping skills.

After God decided to call my mom home it felt like she had a personal talk with him and said, "Please send my daughter a husband." Three months after she passed away, I started dating my husband who had been my coworker for the last five years. I never even looked his way or had any idea he was looking my way. I recall one day having a conversation with another coworker about what we were looking for in a potential mate and he was giving us some feedback and apparently taking notes. Who would have thought my future husband was sitting a few computers down from me and saving lives with me all while listening to me vent about my poor dating life.

He was so patient, kind, quiet, respectful, and sure of what he wanted and what he had to offer. There was no confusion. I often wonder did God say OK now you're ready or did my mom say please help my child. Maybe it was a divine intervention but either way I'm grateful for my husband. The timing was perfect, I needed him! He was extremely supportive of my daughter. He actually drove her to prom when things didn't work out the way we had planned. He went with me to drive her to school at Alabama State and took me to see my father while we were there. We dated for two years, he proposed November 16, 2020, and we got married May 28, 2022. My dad passed away on May 15, 2024. My grandmother was unsure of the arrangements because he didn't have insurance plus, she stated she didn't believe in funerals. The funeral home told me I couldn't see his body until she decided. She told me she would notify me once she figured everything out. She decided to bury him the day before my wedding. As I was traveling back to my hotel room on May 27, 2022, I received a text from my cousin in Alabama with pictures of my father in a casket: **He looks so peaceful I figured no one updated you.**

So, what should have been the happiest day of my life was a beautiful, painful roller coaster of emotions. Although my mom or dad wasn't there with me physically, I felt like she sent my husband my way and it was her final gift to me and my dad said take care of my baby, she's yours now.

I debated about writing this book because I thought to myself, *Shanta some if not most people could care less about your childhood trauma/struggles.* Also, who's to say that my trauma is even seen as valid. Who cares that you have mommy and daddy issues and suffer with anxiety and depression? Anxiety isn't even that bad everyone has anxiety, right? Someone actually told me this before. Then one could say your childhood/life wasn't that bad, was it? I know people who have dealt with worse! You seem fine to me! Well yes and no.

Yes, everyone has dealt with anxiety at some point, but did it become a disorder, chronic, and affect you daily? No, my childhood/life wasn't that bad I've seen and heard of worse myself. However, it's not healthy to compare trauma to trauma. Trauma by definition is a deeply distressing or disturbing experience, any experience which calls up distressing affects such as freight, anxiety, shame, or physical pain may operate as trauma (Krystal, 2015).

When someone gives a testimony in church do we compare what God has done for them to others? What may seem small and insignificant to one person could be a huge blessing for others. That's like one person standing up and saying they just closed on their new four-bedroom home and another person just got their first one-bedroom apartment. Well, to some that apartment might not seem so great and worth the testimony. What if I told you that person was homeless prior to this or maybe they left an abusive relationship and now they are able to finally get on their feet, which by the way it really doesn't matter they both were blessed! We are all guilty of comparing our lives to others and social media has made it worse! But trauma is trauma, a struggle is a struggle, and a testimony is a testimony. Don't minimize your blessing nor your pain. I did this for years and didn't even realize it. It's all valid!!

My daughter actually had her own struggle with her mental health. She was battling depression. I could tell something was wrong and she also felt comfortable enough to confide in me that something felt wrong. She said, "Mom, I think I'm depressed, and I want help." We got on the internet, looked at a few therapists, and read their bios, and she chose the one she felt would be a good match for her. She asked me about my mental health and if I ever thought about suicide. I was honest with her and very transparent. It had crossed my mind at one point. As an attempt to help her, I also let her read what I had written so far doing the writing of this book. I told her I'm not sure whether I would publish it or not. After reading it, she told me, "Mom, you have to!! I have friends that I believe your book can help!" I said, "OK then I will do it!" Well, it took a couple years but here we are.

After the death of my mother, I just started reflecting on everything. My life, her life, my childhood, my adulthood, her illness, and her struggles. Analyzing myself as a woman, a mother, a sister, and my ability to hopefully be someone's wife one day. What can I learn from her life. What did she teach me in the midst of dealing with her own pain? My mother wasn't perfect, and no one is but I know for a fact she did the very best she could. I was her first born and she was only nineteen years old. The same age I was when I became a mother. She was just trying to figure her own life out while dealing with her childhood trauma and suddenly becoming responsible for another human being. It made me think of myself as a young mother. The mental state I was once in made it difficult to function day to day and still be responsible for a child.

As a mother, we have to set our own feelings aside to care for someone else and provide for them. I don't know a lot about my mother's childhood except for what she told me that day while sitting on the edge of my bed. However, that was enough to know my mother and I were just alike. I remember telling her that one day and she replied, "I wouldn't go that far now but there are similarities." The only difference is honestly she was a lot stronger than I am, very vocal, and possibly more damaged. She didn't care about hurting people feelings, I actually think she enjoyed it at times. Whereas I hold my pain inside, she allowed hers to be known regardless of how it came out. I suffered in silence to allow others to have peace and she said if I don't have any peace neither will you!!! That's what made her a fighter not only physically but in spirit as well. If she did sweat or have any type of fear no one saw it. She didn't allow it to overtake her. Not even breast cancer!! She did the best she could as a mother with the tools life gave her. She used to say, "Sickness is a state of mind and you going to school." That's exactly how she approached the cancer. She was so used to fighting, cancer was no different. She fought up until her last breath.

I regret so deeply wasting time when it came to my mother. It was so much more I could have done, and I should have said. I was so focused on my own pain I feel like I neglected hers. My mother had been who she was all my life; she never switched up. I just wish I could've accepted that sooner than later. I wish we could've gone to therapy together. I wish I would've given her the biggest hug and kiss that day she apologized. I wish I would've verbalized I forgave her and I knew she did the best she could. I also would've validated her trauma and her pain. Although I never disrespected her, I wish I would've been kinder, gave her grace, more understanding, more compassionate and more attention.

I realized afterward that everything worked out according to God's plan and here I was ranting and raving about me. It was never about me. Not getting the funds for nursing school was not about me. Not even the purchase of my home. God didn't bless me with that house for myself, it was always for my mother! For months, every house I put an offer on was denied! During my search I was moving further and further to the west suburbs and that wasn't a part of God's plan. I had given up on my house search and told my realtor I think I'm just going to hold off until next year. Then while visiting my mother in Atlanta that year, I saw a house in an area not far from where we used to live. They were having an open house the day of my return home from Atlanta. I called my best friend and asked her to go with me to view the house. We did and I immediately fell in love with it! There were so many people at the open house, but I told myself this is going to be my last try.

I called my realtor gave him the address and said put in an offer. He did just that and a couple of days went by. The house had multiple offers on it, and they asked for your best and final offer due by the next business day. I offered $17,000 over the asking price and still was denied. I was done looking and trying. That was my last offer! A month later my realtor contacted me and said that the offer fell through, and they contacted him wanting to accept my offer and of course I said yes! This home was a ten-minute drive from the cancer center that my mom was going to. So, when I tell you this house was chosen for her, and I didn't even know it, that's what I meant.

I believe God gave me the opportunity to spend her last days with her. He knew we both needed some form of healing to take place between the two of us, and it did. To this day, I cannot imagine the level of pain I would be enduring had I not had that opportunity. So even when it seems like things are chaotic and you are uncomfortable and bothered, keep the faith; you just never know why God allow things to happen the way he does. Yes, my mother is gone but I'm so grateful I was allowed to say goodbye.

I started writing this book in 2018 and it originated from a journal I started in 2014 after a difficult heartbreak during a time in my life when I was struggling heavily with depression and anxiety. I remained constant with journaling up until September of 2018. For four years I journaled about my life, my struggles, my fears, and my downfalls. I was able to see the highs and lows of my mental health journey and my life in general. As you now know writing has always provided a sense of peace and clarity for me.

Before the pandemic of 2020, I felt as though mental health wasn't discussed as openly as it is right now and that's why I started to tell my own story. I decided to put it in book form with the hopes of helping others like me. I wrote this book as a healing path for me. I also wrote it for anyone that has struggled with their mental health and felt alone or misunderstood. Telling my story and doing some self-reflection on my childhood going into adulthood has been extremely therapeutic as well as analyzing the decisions I've made over time, examining how it all has played a role in my mental health journey. Although some parts of this book are embarrassing, I wanted others to know it was okay that they may be struggling with their mental health. So, I had to piece the whole story together. The good, the bad, and the unpleasant. I want everyone to know it's okay to seek help that involves therapy, medication, or both. What's not okay is for you to ignore it and just pray it gets better. Of course, prayer works but you might just need a prescription as well! Faith, therapy, and medication can all coexist together. Just because you choose to get the medical help that you need does not mean your faith in God is nonexistent nor has it wavered. It's the opposite. Faith without work is dead so do the work. James 2: 14-26 says, "What good is faith without deeds or work? Faith alone unaccompanied by action is dead." Yes, I have faith that God is who he says he is. I pray for peace over my mind and my heart. God has granted me the wisdom to know that there's work to be done. He has placed people in position to help you to achieve whatever you need and desire. That includes your mental health. There are so many faces, levels, and stories to mental illness. I'm just sharing mine.

I pray this book reaches as many hearts as possible. I pray that it ignites the healing process for those that are not only struggling with their mental health but childhood traumas and emotional distress. I pray that it starts the healing process in families and breaks generational curses. I pray that it restores relationships and friendships. Last but not least, I pray that it helps others to recognize warning signs of an unhealthy mental state in themselves and others! And as always, be kind!

RESOURCES

Suicide and crisis Lifeline:
Call or text #988

Substance Abuse and Mental Health Services Administration (SAMHSA):
https://findtreatment.samhsa.gov
or Helpline 1-800-662- HELP (4357)

National Alliance on Mental Illness affiliate:
https://www.nami.org/findsupport

Thank you for reading *Prayer Works
but I Need a Prescription.*
If you enjoyed this book or found it helpful, please help
spread the word by leaving an online review. Thank you!

KEEP IN TOUCH WITH
RONSHANTA WASHINGTON

Instagram: @ANXIOUSAPPAREL_LLC
Tiktok: @anxiousapparelshop
Shop: https://anxiousapparelshop.com